Little Alleluias

SELECT TITLES ALSO BY MARY OLIVER

POETRY

American Primitive
Dream Work
New and Selected Poems: Volume One
White Pine
Why I Wake Early
New and Selected Poems: Volume Two
Swan
A Thousand Mornings
Dog Songs
Blue Horses
Felicity

PROSE

Blue Pastures
Winter Hours
A Poetry Handbook
Upstream

Little Alleluias

COLLECTED POETRY AND PROSE

Mary Oliver

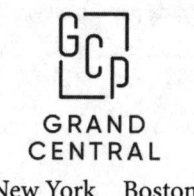

GRAND CENTRAL

New York Boston

Copyright © 2025 by NW Orchard LLC

Cover design by Amanda Kain

Cover photo © Eoghan Kavanagh / Gallery Stock

Cover copyright © 2025 by Hachette Book Group, Inc.

Hachette Book Group supports the right to free expression and the value of copyright. The purpose of copyright is to encourage writers and artists to produce the creative works that enrich our culture.

The scanning, uploading, and distribution of this book without permission is a theft of the author's intellectual property. If you would like permission to use material from the book (other than for review purposes), please contact permissions@hbgusa.com. Thank you for your support of the author's rights.

Grand Central Publishing

Hachette Book Group

1290 Avenue of the Americas, New York, NY 10104

grandcentralpublishing.com

@grandcentralpub

First Edition: September 2025

Grand Central Publishing is a division of Hachette Book Group, Inc. The Grand Central Publishing name and logo is a registered trademark of Hachette Book Group, Inc.

The publisher is not responsible for websites (or their content) that are not owned by the publisher.

Grand Central Publishing books may be purchased in bulk for business, educational, or promotional use. For information, please contact your local bookseller or the Hachette Book Group Special Markets Department at special.markets@hbgusa.com.

Print book interior design by Bart Dawson.

The quotation from "Symposium" is from *The Great Dialogues of Plato* by Plato, translated by W. H. D. Rouse, copyright © 1956, renewed 1984 by J. C. G. Rouse. Used in the original edition of *The Leaf and the Cloud* by permission of Dutton Signet, a division of Penguin Putnam, Inc.

Library of Congress Control Number: 2025939558

ISBNs: 978-0-306-83581-0 (trade paperback); 978-0-306-83582-7 (ebook)

Printed in the United States of America

LSC-C

Printing 3, 2025

CONTENTS

Foreword: TRINITY by Natalie Diaz, 2024 / vii

THE LEAF AND THE CLOUD / 1
2000

WHAT DO WE KNOW / 53
2002

LONG LIFE / 127
2004

Notes / 231
Acknowledgments / 235
About the Author / 237

FOREWORD

TRINITY
by Natalie Diaz

What does it mean, say the words, that the earth is beautiful? And what shall I do about it? What is the gift that I should bring to the world? What is the life that I should live?

These are the questions Mary Oliver asks in her essay "Flow," and they feel, as many of her poems and essays do, close to what I was taught about my relationship, as a Mojave and Akimel O'otham woman, to my Mojave desert and Colorado River. We consider each an autonomous living body, having been created by gods or powerful beings and events, as well as themselves existing as creators of the human and nonhuman bodies which become our experience of living. I have always believed that the similarities in which our bodies occur—how the great lime and emerald palm fronds in Hawaii, like my own lungs, rise and fall in a music of wind and exhalation, or how the mesquite trees on my reservation at Fort Mojave taught my people to tap root along the shore of our river or in the sloughs, slaking themselves where water is abundant—are not accidental but are an important relationship of the imagination as well as survival.

It isn't so crazy to believe that this knowledgeable world imagined us itself, from its own values of life. We young human beings learn from this ancestor how to bloom into our existence, in constellation with and alongside the nonhuman beings of the world. Of consequence to one another.

In Mojave, or Makav, our words for *body* and *land* are bound together—land is 'amat, and body is 'iimat. We care for one as we care for the other, which unfolds a complex and rigorously generous relationship between the *I* of the human body and the bodies of other nonhuman, living beings; and the collective *We* who the *I* becomes through intentional practices and rituals of sensuality. The *We* is not only what makes the world but who we each are, as autonomous and individual, in the world, alongside one another. Each relies on the presence and devotion of the other. *I* am of consequence to *You*, *We* are of consequence to all life.

Oliver says as much and more eloquently in her description of the protective yet fragile shell or home of the ice-cream-worm. She says of this "fortification": it is "the sand and of it, yet separate from it." *Of* being the word that becomes the portal through which she invites us into intimate relationship with what is not often thought of as our body and instead is considered a boundary of our body; the gift of being in the world while also being inseparable from the world. She offers to us that there is living, and all the structures and tasks that make a human life successful, and there is also the wildness of life, within us and outside of us, in constant constellation and blur, at once patterned and also mysterious—these poems and prose pieces gift us the world as an accumulation of our experiences—what we know—and also propel us toward another depth of our human experience; those things which we do not yet know about the world, and consequently, about ourselves.

It is not only a matter of observation or description. Oliver writes, *And that is just the point: how the world, moist and bountiful, calls to each of us to make a new and serious response.* Hers is a purposeful language, one that looks not just with attention but with sensual intention, and though awestruck, seeks to hold, even briefly, the unknowns of the energies that make any life. *Little alleluias,* she called her writings. Not meant to define but to praise, to rejoice in the maker and what has been made, to dare be heard as a whisper or a shout in this immense world. Oliver's call to make a new and serious response resounds with June Jordan's belief that, *Poetry means taking control of the / language of your life.* In Oliver's poems, *seeing* is also *feeling* and both become an overwhelm for which language is a slight anodyne or ease.

Alongside framing a poetics of wonder and wander, the writings across this trinity of works give us glimpses into how the world taught Oliver to love, a generosity revealed in what has sometimes been seen as lack. I'm speaking now about her practices of solitude and even loneliness. Rather than resulting in a distant or detached existence, her lifelong solitary practices, which were also her practices of witnessing the natural world and creating poetry, became the practices that connected her to a community of readers and writers and through which she herself was witnessed, by them, as someone who loved and was loved. She tells us of the childhood "houses" she built to be alone in, made of *a cowl, or a dream, or a palace of grass,* and describes them as a symptom of not being social. Yet in these early structures was where her sensual imagination was shaped, where, perhaps, she became the *blue comma* herself—as when she writes, *off to my woods, my ponds, my sun-filled harbor, no more than a blue comma on the map of the world but, to me, the emblem of everything.* These writings too become the small but powerful shifts in time and pace that we need to truly recognize and then appreciate what it means to be alive, to be struck by the life coursing through us the way it courses within our earth—in rivers and light through the leaves, as jellyfish carried or thrashed by a current, through waves of grass and seas murmuring or crashing our ears, even the sting of salt and dune sand and the rush of sun or stars in our eyes. Perhaps those small houses she built were less like protective shields or limits and more like the portals through which she began to hear and construct the devotional language which became the poetics of how we might love our mysterious, wild, and unknown world enough to protect it.

I'll leave you with a moment of love that might have been learned in those small houses as well as they were learned on the oceans, dunes, and shores. Oliver is speaking of her lover, Molly. She is upstairs, and Molly is downstairs, and for the first time in her life, she hears Molly whistle. It is so unexpected that Oliver hollers down to be sure it is Molly whistling and not a visitor in the house. Molly's reply is that, yes, it is she who is whistling, a thing she had done a long time ago and has in that moment learned that she continues to do well. At this point in the poem, Oliver writes of her beloved, *I know her so well, I think. I thought. Elbow and ankle. Mood and desire. Anguish and frolic. Anger too. And the devotions. And for all that, do we even begin to know each other? Who is this I've been living with for thirty years?* Or for an entire life, we might say. What can any of us make of our momentary intimate lives in such an immense world, with equally immense unknowns, mysteries as great as death or the whale, as deep as love or the ocean, as sad and beautiful as a jellyfish torn and glistening in a small fortress of shore rock? This world in which we are of consequence, shaped as violently and tenderly as we also shape it. Marked by and marking. Though we might not always, or ever, know what it means, we can't deny: *the earth, the earth is beautiful.* How lucky to be in it.

Natalie Diaz was born on the Fort Mojave Indian Village in Needles, California, on the banks of the Colorado River. She is Mojave and an enrolled member of the Gila River Indian Tribe (Akimel O'odham). Diaz is the author of *Postcolonial Love Poem*, winner of the Pulitzer Prize in Poetry, finalist for the National Book Award, Forward Prize in Poetry, and *Los Angeles Times* Book Prize, and winner of a Publishing Triangle Award. Her first book, *When My Brother Was an Aztec*, won an American Book Award. She is a MacArthur Foundation Fellow, a Lannan Literary Foundation Fellow, a Native Arts and Culture Foundation Fellow, and a former Princeton University Hodder Fellow.

Diaz was awarded the Princeton Holmes National Poetry Prize and is a member of the Board of Trustees for the United States Artists, where she is an alumnus of the Ford Fellowship. She is founding director of the Center for Imagination in the Borderlands and the Maxine and Jonathan Marshall Chair in Modern and Contemporary Poetry at Arizona State University, where she is a professor in the English MFA program. In 2021, Diaz was elected a chancellor of the Academy of American Poets and was a finalist for the Neustadt International Prize for Literature. She resides in Phoenix, Arizona, but is currently living in Brooklyn as a Mellon Foundation Research Residency Fellowship and a Senior Fellow at the New School Institute on Race, Power, and Political Economy.

Little Alleluias

THE LEAF AND THE CLOUD

A POEM

2000

We have seen that when the earth had to be prepared for the habitation of man, a veil, as it were, of intermediate being was spread between him and its darkness, in which were joined, in a subdued measure, the stability and insensibility of the earth, and the passion and perishing of mankind.

But the heavens, also, had to be prepared for his habitation.

Between their burning light,—their deep vacuity, and man, as between the earth's gloom of iron substance, and man, a veil had to be spread of intermediate being;—which should appease the unendurable glory to the level of human feebleness, and sign the changeless motion of the heavens with a semblance of human vicissitude.

Between the earth and man arose the leaf. Between the heaven and man came the cloud. His life being partly as the falling leaf, and partly as the flying vapour.

—John Ruskin
From *Modern Painters*, vol. v, part vii, ch. 1

CONTENTS

Flare / 5

Work / 12

From The Book of Time / 19

Riprap / 26

Rhapsody / 33

Gravel / 37

Evening Star / 46

Flare

1.

Welcome to the silly, comforting poem.

It is not the sunrise,
which is a red rinse,
which is flaring all over the eastern sky;

it is not the rain falling out of the purse of God;

it is not the blue helmet of the sky afterward,

or the trees, or the beetle burrowing into the earth;

it is not the mockingbird who, in his own cadence,
will go on sizzling and clapping
from the branches of the catalpa that are thick with blossoms,
    that are billowing and shining,
        that are shaking in the wind.

2.

    You still recall, sometimes, the old barn on your great-grandfather's farm, a place you visited once, and went into, all alone, while the grownups sat and talked in the house.

It was empty, or almost. Wisps of hay covered the floor, and some wasps sang at the windows, and maybe there was a strange fluttering bird high above, disturbed, hoo-ing a little and staring down from a messy ledge with wild, binocular eyes.

Mostly, though, it smelled of milk, and the patience of animals; the give-offs of the body were still in the air, a vague ammonia, not unpleasant.

Mostly, though, it was restful and secret, the roof high up and arched, the boards unpainted and plain.

You could have stayed there forever, a small child in a corner, on the last raft of hay, dazzled by so much space that seemed empty, but wasn't.

Then—you still remember—you felt the rap of hunger—it was noon—and you turned from that twilight dream and hurried back to the house, where the table was set, where an uncle patted you on the shoulder for welcome, and there was your place at the table.

3.

Nothing lasts.
There is a graveyard where everything I am talking about is,
now.

I stood there once, on the green grass, scattering flowers.

4.

Nothing is so delicate or so finely hinged as the wings
of the green moth
against the lantern

against its heat
against the beak of the crow
in the early morning.

Yet the moth has trim, and feistiness, and not a drop
 of self-pity.

Not in this world.

5.

My mother
was the blue wisteria,
my mother
was the mossy stream out behind the house,
my mother, *alas, alas,*
did not always love her life,
heavier than iron it was
as she carried it in her arms, from room to room,
oh, unforgettable!

I bury her
in a box
in the earth
and turn away.
My father
was a demon of frustrated dreams,
was a breaker of trust,
was a poor, thin boy with bad luck.
He followed God, there being no one else
he could talk to;
he swaggered before God, there being no one else
who would listen.

Listen,
this was his life.
I bury it in the earth.
I sweep the closets.
I leave the house.

6.

I mention them now,
I will not mention them again.

It is not lack of love
nor lack of sorrow.
But the iron thing they carried, I will not carry.

I give them—one, two, three, four—the kiss of courtesy,
    of sweet thanks,
of anger, of good luck in the deep earth.
May they sleep well. May they soften.

But I will not give them the kiss of complicity.
I will not give them the responsibility for my life.

7.

Did you know that the ant has a tongue
with which to gather in all that it can
of sweetness?

Did you know that?

8.

The poem is not the world.
It isn't even the first page of the world.

But the poem wants to flower, like a flower.
It knows that much.

It wants to open itself,
like the door of a little temple,
so that you might step inside and be cooled and refreshed,
and less yourself than part of everything.

9.

The voice of the child crying out of the mouth of the
    grown woman
is a misery and a disappointment.
The voice of the child howling out of the tall, bearded,
    muscular man
is a misery, and a terror.

10.

Therefore, tell me:
what will engage you?
What will open the dark fields of your mind,
    like a lover
        at first touching?

11.

Anyway,
there was no barn.
No child in the barn.

No uncle no table no kitchen.

Only a long lovely field full of bobolinks.

12.

When loneliness comes stalking, go into the fields, consider
the orderliness of the world. Notice
something you have never noticed before,

like the tambourine sound of the snow-cricket
whose pale green body is no longer than your thumb.

Stare hard at the hummingbird, in the summer rain,
shaking the water-sparks from its wings.

Let grief be your sister, she will whether or no.
Rise up from the stump of sorrow, and be green also,
    like the diligent leaves.

A lifetime isn't long enough for the beauty of this world
and the responsibilities of your life.

Scatter your flowers over the graves, and walk away.
Be good-natured and untidy in your exuberance.

In the glare of your mind, be modest.
And beholden to what is tactile, and thrilling.

Live with the beetle, and the wind.

This is the dark bread of the poem.
This is the dark and nourishing bread of the poem.

Work

1.

I am a woman sixty years old and of no special courage.
Everyday—a little conversation with God, or his envoy
    the tall pine, or the grass-swimming cricket.
Everyday—I study the difference between water and stone.
Everyday—I stare at the world; I push the grass aside
    and stare at the world.

The spring pickerel in the burn and shine of the tight-
    packed water;
the sweetness of the child on the shore; also, its
    radiant temper;
the snail climbing the morning glories, carrying
    his heavy wheel;
the green throats of the lilies turning from the wind.
This is the world.

Comes the hunter under the red leaves;
come the hounds, on their stubbies;
like wind they pour through the grass,
like wind they pour up the hill;
like wind they twist and swirl in the long grass.

Everyday—I have work to do:
I feel my body rising through the water
                not much more than a leaf;
and I feel like the child, crazed by beauty
                or filled to bursting with woe;
and I am the snail in the universe of the leaves
                trudging upward;
and I am the pale lily who believes in God,
                though she has no word for it,

and I am the hunter, and I am the hounds,
and I am the fox, and I am the weeds of the field,
and I am the tunnel and the coolness under the earth,
and I am the pawprint in the dust,
I am the dusty toad who looks up unblinking
and sees (do you also see them?) the white clouds
in their blind, round-shouldered haste;

    I am a woman sixty years old, and glory is my work.

2.

The dreamy heads of the grass in early summer.
In midsummer: thick and heavy.
Sparrows swing on them, they bend down.
When the sparrow sings, its whole body trembles.

Later, the pollen shakes free.
Races this way and that way,
like a mist full of life, which it is.
We stand at the edge of the field, sneezing.
We praise God, or Nature, according to our determinations.

Then the grass curls or breaks, or we cut it.
What does it matter?
Do you think the grass is growing so wild and thick
    for its own life?
Do you think the cutting is the ending, and not, also,
    a beginning?
This is the world.

The pink globes of the peonies
open under the sun's early-morning hands.

The vine of the honeysuckle
perks upward—
the fine-hold of its design
did not need to be so wonderful, did it?
but is.

This is the world.

The bat squeaks.
The bat leans down out of dark July
with his elf's face.

The twenty-winged cloud of yellow butterflies
floats into the field.
The mustard-heads bend under their soft weight.

This is the world.

    3.

Would it be better to sit in silence?
To think everything, to feel everything, to say nothing?

This is the way of the orange gourd.
This is the habit of the rock in the river, over which
    the water pours all night and all day.
But the nature of man is not the nature of silence.
Words are the thunders of the mind.
Words are the refinement of the flesh.
Words are the responses to the thousand curvaceous moments—
    we just manage it—
      sweet and electric, words flow from the brain
      and out the gate of the mouth.

We make books of them, out of hesitations and grammar.
We are slow, and choosy.
This is the world.

4.

All day I have been pining for the past.
That's when the big dog, Luke, breathed at my side.
Then she dashed away then she returned
in and out of the swales, in and out of the creeks,
her dark eyes snapping.
Then she broke, slowly,
in the rising arc of a fever.

And now she's nothing
except for mornings when I take a handful of words
and throw them into the air
so that she dashes up again out of the darkness,

like this—

this is the world.

5.

The green pea
climbs the stake
on her sugary muscles.

The rosy comma of the radish
fattens in the soil.

Farmers call to the white oxen, together they pull the plow.
Girls sigh upward against the bodies of young men.
The century plant opens at last in the frail moonlight.

6.

And how shall we speak of love
except in the splurge of roses, and the long body
    of the river
shining in its silk and froth;

and what could be more wonderful
than the agility and the reaching of the fingers of Hannah,
who is only seven days old;

and what could be more comforting than to fold grief
like a blanket—
to fold anger like a blanket,
with neat corners—
to put them into a box of words?

7.

It may be the rock in the field is also a song.
And it may be the ears of corn swelling under their
    green sleeves
are also songs.
And it may be the river glancing and leaning against
    the dark stone is also a deliberate music.

So I will write my poem, but I will leave room for the world.
I will write my poem tenderly and simply, but
    I will leave room for the wind combing the grass,
for the feather falling out of the grouse's fan-tail,
    and fluttering down, like a song.

And I will sing for the bones of my wrists,
    supple and exemplary.
And the narrow paths of my brain, its lightnings and issues,
    its flags, its ideas.
And the mystery of the number 3.

I will sing for the iron doors of the prison,
and for the broken doors of the poor,
and for the sorrow of the rich, who are mistaken and lonely,

and I will sing for the white dog forever tied up in the orchard,
and I will sing for the morning sun and its panels
    of pink and green on the quiet water,
and for the loons passing over the house.

I will sing for the spirit of Luke.
I will sing for the ghost of Shelley.
I will sing for the Jains and their careful brooms.

I will sing for the salt and the pepper in their little towers
    on the clean table.
I will sing for the rabbit that has crossed our yard
    in the moonlight,
stopping twice to stamp the cold ground
    with his narrow foot.

I will sing for the two coyotes who came at me with their strong
    teeth
and then, at the last moment, began to smile.

I will sing for the veil that never lifts.
I will sing for the veil that begins, once in a lifetime,
    maybe, to lift.
I will sing for the rent in the veil.
I will sing for what is in front of the veil, the
    floating light.
I will sing for what is behind the veil—
    light, light, and more light.

This is the world, and this is the work of the world.

From The Book of Time

1.

I rose this morning early as usual, and went to my desk.
But it's spring,

and the thrush is in the woods,
somewhere in the twirled branches, and he is singing.

And so, now, I am standing by the open door.
And now I am stepping down onto the grass.

I am touching a few leaves.
I am noticing the way the yellow butterflies
move together, in a twinkling cloud, over the field.

And I am thinking: maybe just looking and listening
is the real work.

Maybe the world, without us,
is the real poem.

2.

For how many years have you gone through the house
    shutting the windows,
while the rain was still five miles away

and veering, o plum-colored clouds, to the north,
away from you

and you did not even know enough
to be sorry,

you were glad
those silver sheets, with the occasional golden staple,

were sweeping on, elsewhere,
violent and electric and uncontrollable—

and will you find yourself finally wanting to forget
all enclosures, including

the enclosure of yourself, o lonely leaf, and will you
dash finally, frantically,

to the windows and haul them open and lean out
to the dark, silvered sky, to everything

that is beyond capture, shouting
I'm here, I'm here! Now, now, now, now, now.

3.

I dreamed
I was traveling

from one country
to another

jogging
on the back
of a white horse
whose hooves

were the music
of dust and gravel
whose halter
was made of the leafy braids

of flowers,
whose name
was Earth.
And it never

grew tired
though the sun
went down
like a thousand roses

and the stars
put their white faces
in front of the black branches
above us

and then
there was nothing around us
but water
and the white horse

turned suddenly
like a bolt of white cloth

opening
under the cloth-cutter's deft hands

and became
a swan.
Its red tongue
flickered out

as it perceived
my great surprise
my huge and unruly pleasure
my almost unmanageable relief....

4.

" 'Whoever shall be guided so far towards the mysteries of love, by contemplating beautiful things rightly in due order, is approaching the last grade. Suddenly he will behold a beauty marvellous in its nature, that very Beauty, Socrates, for the sake of which all the earlier hardships had been borne: in the first place, everlasting, and never being born nor perishing, neither increasing nor diminishing; secondly, not beautiful here and ugly there, not beautiful now and ugly then, not beautiful in one direction and ugly in another direction, not beautiful in one place and ugly in another place. Again, this beauty will not show itself like a face or hands or any bodily thing at all, nor as a discourse or a science, nor indeed as residing in anything, as in a living creature or in earth or heaven or anything else, but being by itself with itself always in simplicity; while all the beautiful things elsewhere partake of this beauty in such manner, that when *they* are born and perish *it* becomes neither less nor more and nothing at all happens to it....' "

5.

What secrets fly out of the earth
when I push the shovel-edge,
when I heave the dirt open?

And if there are no secrets
what is that smell that sweetness rising?

What is my name,
o what is my name
that I may offer it back
to the beautiful world?

Have I walked
long enough
where the sea breaks raspingly
all day and all night upon the pale sand?

Have I admired sufficiently the little hurricane
of the hummingbird?

the heavy
thumb
of the blackberry?

the falling star?

6.

Count the roses, red and fluttering.
Count the roses, wrinkled and salt.
Each with its yellow lint at the center.

Each with its honey pooled and ready.
Do you have a question that can't be answered?
Do the stars frighten you by their heaviness
    and their endless number?
Does it bother you, that mercy is so difficult to
    understand?
For some souls it's easy; they lie down on the sand
    and are soon asleep.
For others, the mind shivers in its glacial palace,
    and won't come.
Yes, the mind takes a long time, is otherwise occupied
than by happiness, and deep breathing.
Now, in the distance, some bird is singing.
And now I have gathered six or seven deep red,
    half-opened cups of petals between my hands,
and now I have put my face against them
and now I am moving my face back and forth, slowly,
    against them.
The body is not much more than two feet and a tongue.
Come to me, says the blue sky, and say the word.
And finally even the mind comes running, like a wild thing,
    and lies down in the sand.
Eternity is not later, or in any unfindable place.
Roses, roses, roses, roses.

7.

Even now
I remember something

the way a flower
in a jar of water

remembers its life
in the perfect garden

the way a flower
in a jar of water

remembers its life
as a closed seed

the way a flower
in a jar of water

steadies itself
remembering itself

long ago
the plunging roots

the gravel the rain
the glossy stem

the wings of the leaves
the swords of the leaves

rising and clashing
for the rose of the sun

the salt of the stars
the crown of the wind

the beds of the clouds
the blue dream

the unbreakable circle.

Riprap

1.

Upon the rocks grow beautiful, small things.
Mussels, with mossy beards.
Dark blue shells.

They sigh as the tide rises.

Starfish cruise and cling.
Bluefish plunge and leap, their long bodies swirl,
    their teeth are uncountable.
The tides rise, the blue sprawl and polish climbs the rocks
    and is momentarily held there.
The loggerhead with her pink parrot's head
    feasts among the mussels.
Daylight descends slowly, and the *now* that is a day
    becomes the *now* that is the night,
the white moon the only boat,
the white heron the only fisherman left on the black rocks.

2.

In my mind, the arguers never stop—
the skeptic and the amazed—

the general and the particular, in their
    uneasy relationship.

Then the robin sings.

Then the bulb of the lily becomes the stalk,
the stalk opens into a handkerchief of white light.

O what is beauty
that I should be up at
four A.M. trying to arrange this
thick song?
What is beauty that I should
bow down in the fields of the world, as though
someone, somewhere,
made it?

O, what is beauty
that I feel it to be so hot-blooded and suggestive,
so filled with imperative

beneath the ease of its changes,
between the leaves and the clouds of its thousand
    and again a thousand opportunities?

    3.

The sweet-faced cat,
the good goat,
the golden feet of the hen—
    the sealed jug of her egg—

the black mole's long-knuckled hands,
the spears of the grass,
    the sun on everyone's back, yours and mine.

Also the poem on the page,
also the painting on the white wall;
also the instruments and the arms holding them
    and the voices issuing from them.

The turnip, the cabbage, the crook-necked squash;
the three blue bowls;
the fork and the knife.

The sailboat,
the dragger swaying above its heavy nets,
the pink dory crossing the bay with two boys and a dog.

I'm never sure
which part of this dream is me
and which part is the rest of the world.

Therefore.

    4.

Every morning I wake, dress in the dark, go downstairs.
I look out of every window.
I go out and stand on the lawn.
In the east, the slightest light begins
    flinging itself upward
and my heart beats (never an exception) with excitement.
(My gratitude to you, dear heart!)

Though it will all vanish utterly, and surely in
 a little while,
I know what is wonderful—
I know what to hoard in my heart more than the value
 of pearls and seeds.
There was the day you first spoke my name.
There was a white house at the edge of the harbor.
There was the swan, and the hummingbird.
There was music, and paper, and the tirelessly pursued work.
There were a thousand and again a thousand unforgettable days.

And still I'm looking at everything—
in the wide morning and the strike of noon
I'm humming, and clapping my hands,
and I can't stop
not for any reason
not even for the easiest thought.

And, anyway, what is thought
but elaborating, and organizing?
What is thought
but doubting, and crying out?

5.

(In the dark, in the distance,
I can just see the heron
dimpling then calming her long wings.)

6.

As reliable as anything you will ever know,
time moves its dim, heavy thumb over the shoreline

making its changes, its whimsical variations.
Yes, yes, the body never gets away from the world,
its endless granular shuffle and exchange—

everything is one, sooner or later—
the red fox and the bullrush,
the industrious ant and the sleepy bear,
the green crab and the minnow,
the pink boat and the dog in the pink boat,

Shelley's body and the gleaming sand.

When the praying mantis opens its wings
    it becomes a green flower.
When the egg breaks
    it becomes a bird.
When the river is finished, its avenues of light
fold and drop and fall into
and become the sea.

Therefore.

7.

But what is it then that sits in my heart,
that breathes so quietly, and without lungs—
that is here, here in this world, and yet not here?

8.

Does the body have a soul?
Does the weedy mussel clinging to the rocks have
    a soul?

Does the black snake, sliding along, perking up
the black lump of its head, does it have a soul?

The body has a soul.

What about the butterfly, the tree root?

The butterfly, the tree root.

Is the wren proof?
And the bed of new lilies just opening,
all silk and spit, is it also proof?

The wren, and the lilies.

Does the grain of sand
know it is a grain of sand?
Will secrets fly out of me
when I break open?
Are the stars standing
in any order?
Is supplication
useful?

Exactly.

9.

Now, in the dark, the white heron
strokes the air over the salt marsh, then she

dangles the forks of her feet and her long legs and comes
floating down to the rocks. She shakes herself, just once,

so that her body for an instant is a white fire—
not herself but the perfection of self,

a white fire.
If I look carefully I can see it.

Then the yellow eye moves, she arches forward slightly
and stares into the moving water,

10.

and we are back
in this world.

Rhapsody

1.

Gold bead after hot gold bead formed
    on the green tassels until they were
the crest of summer, yellow and orange
    seed-casks, skull-curls, tight, bright,
one might even say rhapsodic—oh!
    the sweetness of reality!

Later I caught him, Time hurrying by, by
    the blue sleeve, and I harangued him
against his foolish claim, that the field is all his,
    that everything is his.

Not so. I was there. In the honey-land.
    And you were there too.
I was there with you.

2.

My brother the fox
goes home to his home
under the red roses.

The muskrat
sinks
with a rippling happiness
in the dark water.

(He has sharp teeth, the color of corn.
Though once he did me great harm
I forgive him.
And hope he forgives me.)

The bluebird
is dropping the pearls of his song
out of the sky.

The ant
is sleeping
inside his pale
delicately tunneled hill.

3.

I am so busy among
Shelley's long poems, Plato, Godwin's
Enquiry, Carlyle concerning
the failed revolution that bloody sorrow, and,
as always, Emerson.

Now and again, of course, I look up; a person must.
Maybe I eat an apple or a pear.
Maybe I walk out with the happy dogs.
Maybe I come back into the house, calling your name.

Or maybe you whisper mine.

4.

Have you seen the roses shiver then open their small fluted
    perfect panels of mildest silk, besieged
by another idea? Have you seen their wild faces
    when they first open?

Have you seen them lifting themselves to the
    heat of the sun,
or the rain tapping with its slender fingers on
    the pale sand below?
Or the bunched bee in the blossoms, doing its work,
    entering and emerging, and the flowers
shining in their bed of leaves?

5.

Bless the fingers,
for they are as darting as fire.
Bless the little hairs of the body,
for they are softer than grass.
Bless the hips
for they are cunning beyond all other machinery.
Bless the mouth
for it is the describer.
Bless the tongue
for it is the maker of words.
Bless the eyes
for they are the gifts of the angels,
for they tell the truth.
Bless the shoulders
for they are a strength and a shelter.

Bless the thumb
for when working it has godly grip.
Bless the feet
for their knuckles and their modesty.
Bless the spine
for it is the whole story.

6.

Because there is no substitute for vigorous and exact
description, I would like to say how
your eyes, at twilight, reflect, at the same
time, the beauty of the world, and its crimes.

7.

If you are in the garden, I will dress myself in leaves.
If you are in the sea I will slide into that
smooth blue nest, I will talk fish, I will adore salt.
But if you are sad, I will not dress myself in desolation.
I will present myself with all the laughters I can muster.
And if you are angry I will come, calm and steady, with
some small and easy story.

Promises, promises, promises! The tongue jabbers, the heart
strives, fails, strives again. The world is perfect.
Love, however, is an opera, a history, a long walk, that
includes falling and rising, falling and rising, while
the heart stays as sweet as a peach, as radiant and
grateful as the deep-leaved hills.

Gravel

1.

When death
carts me off to the bottomlands,
when I begin
the long work of rising—

Death, whoever and whatever you are, tallest king of
tall kings, grant me these wishes: unstring my bones;
let me be not one thing but all things, and wondrously
scattered; shake me free from my name. Let the wind, and
the wildflowers, and the catbird never know it. Let
time loosen me like the bead of a flower from its wrappings
of leaves. Let me begin the changes, let me—

Can you imagine a world without certainty?
The wind rises the wind falls.

> The gravels of the world,
> the stones of the world
> are in their proper places.

       The vast, writhing
       worms of the sea
       are in their places.

       The white gulls
       on the wet rocks
       are in their places.

       All is certainty.

   2.

Ben sluices through the ferns, hound-smart.
The bracken up to his neck.
He breaks from the wood and gallops over the field.
The sass of his voice rises—

       (Death that slow swim,
       death that long walk over the dunes,
       death that bleached clamshell . . .)

and the rabbits scatter.

       (Oh, heart, I would not dangle you down into
           the sorry places,
       but there are things there as well
           to see, to imagine.)

   3.

Even the mosquito's
    dark dart,

flashing and groaning;
    even the berries, softening back
into the black bog;
    even the wood duck's
white-circled eye,

and the first white lilies
on the shaggy pond,

and the big owl, shaking herself
out of the pitchpines,

even the turtle scratching in the dust,
even the black ant, climbing the mile-high hill,

even the little chattering swift
diving down into the black chimney.

Everything is participate.
Everything is a part of the world
    we can see, taste, touch, hold onto,

and then it is dust.
Dust at last.
Dust and gravel.

(In the distance, the rabbit-field.
Ben—his face in the grass, his chomping.
His sweet, wild eyes.)

4.

Are you afraid?
>The ear of corn knows whereof it is plucked.

Are you afraid?
>The wind moves this way and that way, something
>>is pushing it.

Are you afraid?
>Somewhere a thousand swans are flying
>>through the winter's worst storm.

They are white and shining, their black beaks
>open a little, the red tongues flash.

Now, and *now,* and *now,* and *now* their heavy wings
>rise and fall as they move across the sky.

5.

Goodbye to the goldfinches
in their silver baskets.
Goodbye to the pilot whales, and the curl of their spines
in the crisp waves.
Goodbye to the grasshopper.
Goodbye to the pond lilies, the turtle with her
cat's head.
Goodbye to the lion's mane floating in the harbor
like a spangled veil.

Goodbye to the moon uprising in the east.
Goodbye to the going forth, and coming home.

Goodbye to the going forth, and holding on, and worrying.
Goodbye to the engine of breath.

The knee sings its anguish.
The ears fill with the sound of ringing water.
The muscles of the eyes pull toward sleep.

Goodbye to the swaying trees.
Goodbye to the black triangles of the winter sea.
Goodbye to oranges, the prick of their fragrance.
Goodbye to the fox sparrow,
goodbye to the blue-winged teal.
Goodbye to lettuce, and the pale turnip,
and the gatherings of the rice fields.
Goodbye to the morning light.
Goodbye to the goldfinches
            and their wavering songs.

Slowly
up the hill,
like a thicket of white flowers,
forever
is coming.

6.

It is the nature of stone
to be satisfied.
It is the nature of water
to want to be somewhere else.

Everywhere we look:
the sweet guttural swill of the water
tumbling.
Everywhere we look:
the stone, basking in the sun,

or offering itself
to the golden lichen.

It is our nature not only to see
that the world is beautiful

but to stand in the dark, under the stars,
or at noon, in the rainfall of light,

frenzied,
wringing our hands,

half-mad, saying over and over:

what does it mean, that the world is beautiful—
what does it mean?

The child asks this,
and the determined, laboring adult asks this—

both the carpenter and the scholar ask this,
and the fisherman and the teacher;

both the rich and the poor ask this
(maybe the poor more than the rich)

and the old and the very old, not yet having figured it out,
    ask this
desperately

standing beside the golden-coated field rock,
or the tumbling water,
or under the stars—

what does it mean?
what does it mean?

7.

The high-piled plum-colored storm-heavy clouds
are approaching.
The fly mumbles against the glass.

This is the world.

The hot little bluebirds in the box are getting ready to fly.
This is the world.

The sweet in the parsnip
waits for our praise.

The dragonfly lives its life
without a single error, it also
waits for our praise.

The pale-green moths are pressing
against the screen, fluttering, they are
dying to get in to press their papery bodies
into the light.

This is the world.

8.

Listen, I don't think we're going to rise
in gauze and halos.
Maybe as grass, and slowly.
Maybe as the long-leaved, beautiful grass

I have known, and you have known—
or the pine trees—
or the dark rocks of the zigzag creek
    hastening along—

or the silver rain—

or the hummingbird.

9.

I look up
into the faces of the stars,
into their deep silence.

10.

This is the poem of goodbye.
And this is the poem of don't know.

My hands touch the lilies
then withdraw;

my hands touch the blue iris
then withdraw;

and I say, not easily but carefully—
the words round in the mouth, crisp on the tongue—

dirt, mud, stars, water—
I know you as if you were myself.
How could I be afraid?

Evening Star

    1.

Once
in the woods
snake came
like a whip
like a piece of a circle
like black water
flowing down the hill.
"Watch me,"
it whispered—
then poured
like black water
through the field—
then hurried down,
like black water,
into the mouse's hole.

And out of this
you might draw
the thinnest of shining threads—

whirl it around and
fling it into the air,
fling it into the air—

again and again it will land on the earth
crimped and cursive,
but spelling nothing,

for, dear God,
we too are down here
in such darkness.

2.

It is easy to fall down on your knees
when the shining rain begins to happen.

It is easy to be thankful
for the bundles of wild roses
ledged along the dune.

It is as easy as if you were yourself a flower in the field,
    the rain tossing you and tossing you,

until you are that flower—
    as torn as muddy as golden as that.

3.

The snake never shuts its eyes.

4.

I have lit candles.
    (Though I am not ready, I am willing.)

I have placed one word next to another
    to build something full of praise.
I have admired the hummingbird, dazzling among the lilies.
Also the tooth of the otter, the compost pile,
    the first star in the evening sky.
        (Though I am not ready, I am simmering.)

5.

And certainly and easily I can see
how God might be one rose bud,
one white feather in the heron's enormous, slowly opening wing.

It's after that
it gets difficult.

6.

The snake never shuts its eyes.
The mouse sits tight.

7.

The good shepherd of the fields, whoever he is,
has so many wonderful and saucy tricks.

I want to find him,
I want to discover just one more trick.

Oh, nobody runs so hard
as the doubters running over the hot fields,

    crying out for faith,
        looking for it in the high places and the low places,
        looking for it everywhere,

oh, see how I run!

    8.

The snake never shuts its eyes.
The mouse sits tight
in the beautiful field.

    9.

I went down all alone, to the black pond.
Slow summer day.
No one around.
Not even a bird singing, not a wind awake, nothing.

Yet nothing could ever convince me
that I was alone.

If God exists he isn't just butter and good luck—
he isn't just the summer day the red rose,

he's the snake he's the mouse,
he's the hole in the ground,

for which thoroughness, if anything, I would adore him,
if I could adore him.

Adore him.

10.

The first streak of light in the darkness,
the first bird to sing,
the first whale to rise out of the black water,
the first morning of the spring tide
the first lupine geranium poppy
first sweet corn,
the first afternoon spent outdoors, after illness,

first child
speaking its first words
first peach on the tree
first grapes
first hand-holding   first kiss

first afternoon of snow
flakes like salt tapping the leaves
then the swirl then the soft clouds tumbling down

first road to the ocean,
first smell of the ocean
first white heron
first abalone,

first crab, iridescent in the seaweed
first mountain
first fern
first egg with a tapping from inside

first rose
red rose   first white rose   opening
itself and no more than itself

and more than itself.

11.

The pickerel
swims up from the pond from its roses of slow decay, and
looks at me
astonished.

What is it I need to know?

The gypsy moths, still caterpillars,
wrench themselves from the milky shreds of birth
and set out on the long journey
in the shining tree.

What is it I don't know that I need to know?

12.

Think of me
when you see the evening star.
Think of me when you see the wren
    the flowing root of the creek beneath him,
   dark   silver   and cold

Remember me I am the one who told you
he sings for happiness.
I am the one who told you
that the grass is also alive, and listening.

alleluiah alleluiah
sighs the pale green moth
on the screen door,

alleluiah alleluiah
the red tongues of the white swans
shine out of their black beaks
as they shout
as their wings rise and fall

rise and fall

oh rise and fall

through the raging flowers of the snow.

WHAT DO WE KNOW

POEMS AND PROSE POEMS

2002

"The invisible and imponderable is the sole fact."

—Emerson, *Letters and Social Aims*

"My mind is on fire to understand this most intricate riddle."

—*The Confessions of St. Augustine*

CONTENTS

Summer Poem / 59

One Hundred White-sided Dolphins on a Summer Day / 60

The Word / 62

Mockingbird / 63

The Return / 65

Black Snake / 69

Beauty / 70

The Hummingbird / 72

Stones / 73

Raven with Crows / 74

At Blackwater Pond / 76

Wind / 77

The Roses / 78

You Are Standing at the Edge of the Woods / 79

Sometimes I Am Victorious and Even Beautiful / 81

Lion's Mane / 82

Clam / 84

Heron Rises from the Dark, Summer Pond / 85

On the Flats / 87

On Losing a House / 88

Crows / 92

Last Night the Rain Spoke to Me / 94

The Lark / 96

Gratitude / 98

Oranges / 100

Moonlight / 101

Now Are the Rough Things Smooth / 102

A Settlement / 103

Their Wings / 104

Her Grave, Again / 106

Blue Iris / 111

Walking to Oak-Head Pond, and Thinking of the Ponds I Will Visit in the Next Days and Weeks / 112

Early Snow / 114

At Twilight an Angel / 116

Snow Buntings / 118

Winter at Herring Cove / 119

Tree Sparrows / 121

The Loon / 122

Snowy Night / 123

Mink / 125

Summer Poem

Leaving the house,
I went out to see

the frog, for example,
in her shining green skin;

and her eggs
like a slippery veil;

and her eyes
with their golden rims;

and the pond
with its risen lilies;

and its warmed shores
dotted with pink flowers;

and the long, windless afternoon;
and the white heron

like a dropped cloud,
taking one slow step

then standing awhile then taking
another, writing

her own soft-footed poem
through the still waters.

One Hundred White-sided Dolphins on a Summer Day

1.
Fat,
black, slick,
galloping in the pitch
of the waves, in the pearly

fields of the sea,
they leap toward us,
they rise, sparkling, and vanish, and rise sparkling,
they breathe little clouds of mist, they lift perpetual smiles,

they slap their tails on the waves, grandmothers and grandfathers
enjoying the old jokes,
they circle around us,
they swim with us—

2.
a hundred white-sided dolphins
on a summer day,
each one, as God himself
could not appear more acceptable

a hundred times,
in a body blue and black threading through
the sea foam,
and lifting himself up from the opened

tents of the waves on his fishtail,
to look
with the moon of his eye
into my heart,

3.
and find there
pure, sudden, steep, sharp, painful
gratitude
that falls—

I don't know—either
unbearable tons
or the pale, bearable hand
of salvation

on my neck,
lifting me
from the boat's plain plank seat
into the world's

4.
unspeakable kindness.
It is my sixty-third summer on earth
and, for a moment, I have almost vanished
into the body of the dolphin,

into the moon-eye of God,
into the white fan that lies at the bottom of the sea
with everything
that ever was, or ever will be,

supple, wild, rising on flank or fishtail—
singing or whistling or breathing damply through blowhole
at top of head. Then, in our little boat, the dolphins suddenly gone,
we sailed on through the brisk, cheerful day.

The Word

How wonderful! I speak of the soul and seven people rise from their chairs and leave the room, seven others lean forward to listen. I speak of the body, the spirit, the mockingbird, the hollyhock, leaves opening in the rain, music, faith, angels seen at dusk—and seven more people leave the room and are seen running down the road. Seven more stay where they are but make murmurous disruptive sounds. Another seven hang their heads, feigning disinterest though their hearts are open, their hope is high that they will hear the word even again. The word is already, for them, the song in the forest. They know already how everything is better—the dark trees less terrible, the ocean less hungry—when it comes forth, and looks around with its crisp and lovely eye, and begins to sing.

Mockingbird

Always there is something worth saying
    about glory, about gratitude.
But I went walking a long time across the dunes
    and in all that time spoke not a single word,
nor wrote one down, nor even thought anything at all
    at the window of my heart.

Speechless the snowy tissue of clouds passed over, and more came,
    and speechless they passed also.
The beach plums hung on the hillsides, their branches
    heavy with blossoms; yet not one of them said a word.

And nothing there anyway knew, don't we know, what a word is,
    or could parse down from the general liquidity of feeling
to the spasm and bull's eye of the moment, or the logic,
    or the instance,
trimming the fingernails of happiness, entering the house
    of rhetoric.

And yet there was one there eloquent enough,
    all this time,
and not quietly but in a rhapsody of reply, though with
    an absence of reason, of querulous pestering. The mockingbird
was making of himself
    an orchestra, a choir, a dozen flutes,

a tambourine, an outpost of perfect and exact observation,
    all afternoon rapping and whistling
on the athlete's lung-ful of leafy air. You could not

imagine a steadier talker, hunched deep in the tree,
then floating forth decorative and boisterous and mirthful,
all eye and fluttering feathers. You could not imagine
a sweeter prayer.

The Return

1.

When I went back to the sea
it wasn't waiting.
Neither had it gone away.
All its musics were safe and sound; the circling gulls
were still a commonplace, the fluted shells
rolled on the shore
more beautiful than money—
oh, yes, more beautiful than money!
the thick-necked seals
stood in the salted waves with their soft, untroubled faces
gazing shoreward—

oh bed of silk,
lie back now on your prairies of blackness your fields of sunlight
that I may look at you.

I am happy to be home.

2.

I do not want to be frisky, and theatrical.
I do not want to go forward in the parade of names.
I do not want to be diligent or necessary or in any way
    heavy.

From my mouth to God's ear, I swear it; I want only
    to be a song.

To wander around in the fields like a little reed bird.

To be a song.

3.

Two eggs rolled from the goose nest
    down to the water and halfway into the water.
What good is hoping?
I went there softly, and gathered them
and put them back into the nest

of the goose who bit me hard with her
    lovely black beak with the pink
        tongue-tip quivering,

and beat my arms with her
    lovely long wings
and beat my face with her
    lovely long wings,
what good is trying?
She hissed horribly, wanting me to be frightened.
I wasn't frightened.
I just knew it was over,
those cold white eggs would never hatch,

the birds would forget, soon, and go back
    to the light-soaked pond,
        what good is remembering?

But I wasn't frightened.

4.

Sometimes I really believe it, that I am going to save my life

a little.

5.

When I found the seal pup alone on the far beach,
not sleeping but looking all around, I didn't
reason it out, for reason would have sent me away,
I just
went close but not too close, and lay down on the sand
with my back toward it, and
pretty soon it rolled over, and rolled over
until the length of its body lay along
the length of my body, and so we touched, and maybe
our breathing together was some kind of heavenly conversation
in God's delicate and magnifying language, the one
we don't dare speak out loud,
not yet.

6.

Rumi the poet was a scholar also.
But Shams, his friend, was an angel.
By which I don't mean anything patient or sweet.
When I read how he took Rumi's books and threw them
    into the duck pond,
I shouted for joy. Time to live now,
Shams meant.
               I see him, turning away
casually toward the road, Rumi following, the books
    floating and sinking among the screeching ducks,

oh, beautiful book-eating pond!

7.

The country of the mockingbird is where I now want to be
    thank you, yes.

The days when the snow-white swans might pass over the dunes
are the days I want to eat now, slowly and carefully
and with gratitude. Thank you.

The hours fresh and tidal are the hours I want to hold
    in the palm of my hand, thank you, yes.

Such grace, thank you!

The gate I want to open now is the one that leads into
    the flower-bed of my mind, thank you, yes.

Every day the slow, fresh wind, thank you, yes.

The wing, in the dark, that touches me.

Thank you.

Yes.

Black Snake

The flat rock in the center of the garden heats up every morning in the sun. Black snake coils himself there neatly. He has cousins who have teeth that spring up and down and are full of the sap of death, but what of that, so have we all. As for his sporting life, there are many things he can do and I have seen a few of them: he can climb a tree and dangle like a red-eyed rope out of its branches; he can swim; he can catch a mouse and swallow it like a soft stone. Also he can lie perfectly still and stare with his lidless eyes in the greatest hope: that you will not notice him. If you do, however, he will lift his chin and extrude the fray of his tongue, which many find frightening. But tell me, if you would praise the world, what is it you would leave out? Besides, he is only hoping that you will let him live his life.

And now that you have seen him, he looks shyly at nothing and streams away into the grass, his long body swaying like a suddenly visible song.

Beauty

When the owl
on her plush and soundless wings
rises
from the black waves

of the oak leaves,
or floats
out of the needles
of the pines

that are moaning,
that are tossing,
I think:
o she is beautiful

with her eyes
like burning moons,
with her feet
like twisted braids

of old gold
flexing and curling—
and I am glad to see her—
some wild loyalty has me

to the root of the heart—
even when she ruffles down
into the field
and jabs like a mad thing

and it's hopeless,
it's also wonderful,
so I thank
whatever made her—

this beast of a bird
with her thick breast
and her shimmering wings—
whose nest, in the dark trees,

is trimmed with screams and bones—
whose beak
is the most terrible cup
I will ever enter.

The Hummingbird

It's morning, and again I am that lucky person who is in it.
And again it is spring,
and there are the apple trees,
and the hummingbird in its branches.
On the green wheel of his wings
he hurries from blossom to blossom,
which is his work, that he might live.

He is a gatherer of the fine honey of promise,
and truly I go in envy
of the ruby fire at his throat,
and his accurate, quick tongue,
and his single-mindedness.

Meanwhile the knives of ambition are stirring
down there in the darkness behind my eyes,
and I should go inside now to my desk and my pages.
But still I stand under the trees, happy and desolate,
wanting for myself such a satisfying coat
and brilliant work.

Stones

The white stones were mountains, then they went traveling.
The pink stones also were part of a mountain before
the glacier's tongue gathered them up.
Now they lie resting under the waves.
The green stones are lovelier than the blue stones, I thought
    for a little while,
then I changed my mind.
Stones born of the sediments tell what ooze floated down
    the outwash once.
Stones born of the fire have red stars inside their bodies,
    and seams of white quartz.
Also I admire the heft, and the circularities
as they lie without wrists or ankles just under the water.
Also I imagine how they lie quietly all night
under the moon and whatever passes overhead—say, the floating
    lily of the night-heron.
It is apparent also how they lie relaxed under the sun's
    golden ladders.
Each one is a slow-wheeler.
Each one is a tiny church, locked up tight.
Each one is perfect—but none of them is ready quite yet
to come to the garden, to raise corn
or the bulb of the iris.
If I lived inland I would want to take one or two home with me
just to look at in that long life of dust and grass,
but I hope I wouldn't.
I hope I wouldn't take even one like a seed from the sunflower's face,
like an ant's white egg from the warm nursery under the hill.
I hope I would leave them, in the perfect balance of things,
in the clear body of the sea.

Raven with Crows

I was just
driving down-hill, in the early morning, when
surprise winged up from the road:
it was

Raven. This is
not a big bird, you understand, but an
impossibly big bird, its
chunky, almost blooming black beak

and its large unquenchable eyes
shine
like a small unheard explosion; it is
no crow, no perky, stiff-winged, head-bobbing

corn-meddler. Over it,
in a tree beside the road,
a dozen such crows gave great complaint,
and if you were a black prince

and lived
in the solitary mountains, and had
just come down
for a look at the village, and the villagers

all milled around you, storming and screaming,
you, too, probably, would be at your best:
silent, gleaming, not threatening but
beautifully acrobatic,

> with an almost jointless ease
> opening your heavy wings over
> their bobbing, worried bodies, or falling
> hawk-wise down air, then scooping
>
> gracefully away,
> not showing off, yet clearly
> an advertisement for the more
> than ordinary life, for the
>
> remembrance
> of the gorgeous and the powerful and the improbable. And then
> it flew off, opening up as it went, to a hugeness unimagined,
> the morning sky.

At Blackwater Pond

The pond is not a temple. The blue heron and the green heron are not the attendants of a temple yard. One of them, in fact, appears to be asleep. The yellow eyes at this moment are looking at nothing, and the little fish in their rainbow shirts are gliding peacefully by. There is an old story, often told, of a warrior frightened before battle, not so much for his own peril but for the strife to come, and the awful taking of life by his own sword. Suddenly a figure appears beside him—it is one of the gods, in the dress of battle and on his face an expression of willingness and ferocity. His speech is brief, and all-encouraging. Now the green heron, that looks like nothing so much as a polished jar waiting for flowers, shifts its body, stretching the dark maroon neck, the wild crown, the yellow legs. And now the blue heron is walking rapidly, one might say devotedly, along the shore. And the water opens willingly for the terrible feet. And the narrow face, the powerful beak, plunge down.

Wind

I am tired of explanations. Unless they are spoken by the best mouths. Black bear coming up from sleep, growling her happiness. Nighthawks snapping their way through the dusk. Or the voice of the wind itself, flailing out of any and every quarter of the sky.

Especially in summer. Especially in the fields, close to the ground. Listen! Let the high branches go on with their opera, it's the song of the fields I wait for, when the sky turns orange and the wind arrives, waving his thousand arms. Or, autumn! I hurry out to the middle of the field and stand where the tough goldenrod, seeded and tasseled, is vigorously tossing—until something thankful rises from my own body. The goldenrod lashes back and forth, each stem on its knuckled foot. Yes! Yes! Yes! And then the dry earth begins to anticipate, and then I fall to my knees, and then the flowers cry out, and then the wind breaks open its silver countries of rain.

The Roses

All afternoon I have been walking over the dunes, hurrying from one thick raft of the wrinkled, salt roses to another, leaning down close to their dark or pale petals, red as blood or white as snow. And now I am beginning to breathe slowly and evenly— the way a hunted animal breathes, finally, when it has galloped, and galloped—when it is wrung dry, but, at last, is far away, so the panic begins to drain from the chest, from the wonderful legs, and the exhausted mind.

Oh sweetness pure and simple, may I join you?

I lie down next to them, on the sand. But to tell about what happens next, truly I need help.

Will somebody or something please start to sing?

You Are Standing at the Edge of the Woods

You are standing at the edge of the woods
at twilight
when something begins
to sing, like a waterfall

pouring down
through the leaves. It is
the thrush.
And you are just

sinking down into your thoughts,
taking in
the sweetness of it—those chords,
those pursed twirls—when you hear

out of the same twilight
the wildest red outcry. It pitches itself
forward, it flails and scabs
all the surrounding space with such authority

you can't tell
whether it is crying out on the
scarp of victory, with its hooked foot
dabbed into some creature that now

with snapped spine
lies on the earth—or whether
it is such a struck body itself, saying
goodbye.

The thrush
is silent then, or perhaps
has flown away.
The dark grows darker.

The moon,
in its shining white blouse,
rises.
And whatever that wild cry was

it will always remain a mystery
you have to go home now and live with,
sometimes with the ease of music, and sometimes in silence,
for the rest of your life.

Sometimes I Am Victorious and Even Beautiful

Sometimes I am victorious and even beautiful—
as when I go down to the pond in the half-light
and wade out into the black water,
where I unloop the taut lines from the willow stakes
    and bend to the weight
and lift the trap from the water—not slowly and carefully
    as in ordinary work, but hard and fast—

and open it,
and stare down and see the turtle's foot-wide mossy shell
and he sees me
    and he thrashes

and I gaze into his pink throat and haul him higher
and he hisses, his eyes shine
and the tongue wags in the gaping, beak-shaped mouth
and I shake him from the trap, his thick head flashing,

    and he swims away

and I close the trap with the heels of my boots, and fling it
into the bullbriar wracked and useless,

and the pink sun rises and sees me, by the black water,
smiling,
    washing my hands.

Lion's Mane

It is
the largest sea jelly in the world.
Rosy as sunset, blurry as spilled blood,

it lives
in the cold, clear, deep water,
its slick, five-foot-wide body-purse

like a drifting temple bell, decorated
with long streamers
flickering and searching

downward.
For all the liveliness of my mind,
I have to work to imagine

its life of gleaming and wandering,
its bulbous, slow, salt comfort—
its terror

when the winds unbuckle the blue
sheets of the waves. I don't know
if it sleeps. I know

there is a mouth somewhere
in the underside of the broad, almost
glowing pouch. And I know that it comes, sometimes,

to disaster—
here, for example, on this summer morning,
in the warm shallows,

it lies motionless, like a daughter of the sun
tossed down, with
no hope of rescue. It is

full of rips and tears,
its bright color drains
outward into the kingdom of shells,

sea worms, crabs, and the other
busy tribes. For fear
of its dozens of crumpled, needled streamers, we

don't move it, we only stare
at the almost watery
flat-tire body. But neither

are we casual. Its red skirt
is ruined, it has become
a terrifying death-gown! and still

what do we know about its unwitnessed
deep-sea life? "Goodbye, brightness,"
you say, and I reach down

and touch, just once, lightly,
the spilled, torn, rosy, chill body that is both
strange, and not strange.

Clam

Each one is a small life, but sometimes long, if its place in the universe is not found out. Like us, they have a heart and a stomach; they know hunger, and probably a little satisfaction too. Do not mock them for their gentleness, they have a muscle that loves being alive. They pull away from the light. They pull *down*. They hold themselves together. They refuse to open.

But sometimes they lose their place and are tumbled shoreward in a storm. Then they pant, they fill with sand, they have no choice but must open the smallest crack. Then the fire of the world touches them. Perhaps, on such days, they too begin the terrible effort of thinking, of wondering *who,* and *what,* and *why.* If they can bury themselves again in the sand they will. If not, they are sure to perish, though not quickly. They also have resources beyond the flesh; they also try very hard not to die.

Heron Rises from the Dark, Summer Pond

So heavy
is the long-necked, long-bodied heron,
always it is a surprise
when her smoke-colored wings

open
and she turns
from the thick water,
from the black sticks

of the summer pond,
and slowly
rises into the air
and is gone.

Then, not for the first or the last time,
I take the deep breath
of happiness, and I think
how unlikely it is

that death is a hole in the ground,
how improbable
that ascension is not possible,
though everything seems so inert, so nailed

back into itself—
the muskrat and his lumpy lodge,
the turtle,
the fallen gate.

And especially it is wonderful
that the summers are long
and the ponds so dark and so many,
and therefore it isn't a miracle

but the common thing,
this decision,
this trailing of the long legs in the water,
this opening up of the heavy body

into a new life: see how the sudden
gray-blue sheets of her wings
strive toward the wind; see how the clasp of nothing
takes her in.

On the Flats

Every day
the sea
proves to be
collapsible—

it goes away
rolling and sighing
heavily
out of the long harbor

to the very horizon.
Barefoot,
we walk out
across that level dampness

until we are very far from shore—
far from our house,
or any house,
stepping upon the moist plain

that is all that is left of the
weight, the flurry, the flung salt,
the flash and the dancing
and the big voice of the sea.

What's real
is the real question,
addressed by us but never
by the happy, go-lucky gulls.

Later,
when the sea has returned
as clean and blue as ever,
and we are back home,

in our yards, on our porches,
how curious to remember ourselves
just looking around
that emptiness,

and how we felt sad
without feeling lost—
or, even, strange—
or, even, bereaved—

the way we stand, sometimes,
in death—
or think we do—
in our purest, wildest thoughts.

On Losing a House

1.

The bumble bees
know where their home is.
They have memorized
every stalk and leaf
of the field.
They fall from the air at
exactly
the right place,
they crawl
under the soft grasses,
they enter
the darkness
humming.

2.

Where will we go
with our table and chairs,
our bed,
our nine thousand books,
our TV, PC, VCR,
our cat
who is sixteen years old?
Where will we put down
our dishes and our blue carpets,
where will we put up
our rose-colored,
rice-paper
shades?

3.

We never saw
such a beautiful house,
though it dipped toward the sea,
though it shook and creaked,
though it said to the rain: come in!
and had a ghost—
at night she rattled the teacups
with her narrow hands,
then left the cupboard open—
and once she slipped—or maybe it wasn't a slip—
and called to our cat, who ran to the empty room.
We only smiled.
Unwise! Unwise!

4.

O, what is money?
O, never in our lives have we thought
about money.
O, we have only a little money.
O, now in our sleep
we dream of finding money.
But someone else
already has money.
Money, money, money.
Someone else
can sign the papers,
can turn the key.
O dark, O heavy, O mossy money.

5.

Amazing
how the rich
don't even
hesitate—up go the
sloping rooflines, out goes the
garden, down goes the crooked,
green tree, out goes the
old sink, and the little windows, and
there you have it—a house
like any other—and there goes
the ghost, and then another, they glide over
the water, away, waving and waving
their fog-colored hands.

6.

Don't tell us
how to love, don't tell us
how to grieve, or what
to grieve for, or how loss
shouldn't sit down like a gray
bundle of dust in the deepest
pockets of our energy, don't laugh at our belief
that money isn't
everything, don't tell us
how to behave in
anger, in longing, in loss, in home-
sickness, don't tell us,
dear friends.

7.

Goodbye, house.
Goodbye, sweet and beautiful house,
we shouted, and it shouted back,
goodbye to you, and lifted itself
down from the town, and set off
like a packet of clouds across
the harbor's blue ring,
the tossing bell, the sandy point—and turned
lightly, wordlessly,
into the keep of the wind
where it floats still—
where it plunges and rises still
on the black and dreamy sea.

Crows

In Japan, in Seattle, in Indonesia—there they were—
each one loud and hungry,
crossing a field, or sitting
above the traffic, or dropping

to the lawn of some temple to sun itself
or walk about on strong legs,
like a landlord. I think
they don't envy anyone or anything—

not the tiger, not the emperor,
not even the philosopher.
Why should they?
The wind is their friend, the least tree is home.

Nor is melody, they have discovered, necessary.
Nor have they delicate palates;
without hesitation they will eat
anything you can think of—

corn, mice, old hamburgers—
swallowing with such hollering and gusto
no one can tell whether it's a brag
or a prayer of deepest thanks. At sunrise, when I walk out,

I see them in trees, or on ledges of buildings,
as cheerful as saints, or thieves of the small job
who have been, one more night, successful—
and like all successes, it turns my thoughts to myself.

Should I have led a more simple life?
Have my ambitions been worthy?
Has the wind, for years, been talking to me as well?
Somewhere, among all my thoughts, there is a narrow path.

It's attractive, but who could follow it?
Slowly the full morning
draws over us its mysterious and lovely equation.
Then, in the branches poling from their dark center,

ever more flexible and bright,
sparks from the sun are bursting and melting on the birds' wings
as, indifferent and comfortable,
they lounge, they squabble in the vast, rose-colored light.

Last Night the Rain Spoke to Me

Last night
the rain
spoke to me
slowly, saying,

what joy
to come falling
out of the brisk cloud,
to be happy again

in a new way
on the earth!
That's what it said
as it dropped,

smelling of iron,
and vanished
like a dream of the ocean
into the branches

and the grass below.
Then it was over.
The sky cleared.
I was standing

under a tree.
The tree was a tree
with happy leaves,
and I was myself,

and there were stars in the sky
that were also themselves
at the moment,
at which moment

my right hand
was holding my left hand
which was holding the tree
which was filled with stars

and the soft rain—
imagine! imagine!
the long and wondrous journeys
still to be ours.

The Lark

And I have seen,
at dawn,
the lark
spin out of the long grass

and into the pink air—
its wings,
which are neither wide
nor overstrong,

fluttering—
the pectorals
ploughing and flashing
for nothing but altitude—

and the song
bursting
all the while
from the red throat.

And then he descends,
and is sorry.
His little head hangs,
and he pants for breath

for a few moments
among the hoops of the grass,
which are crisp and dry,
where most of his living is done—

and then something summons him again
and up he goes,
his shoulders working,
his whole body almost collapsing and floating

to the edges of the world.
We are reconciled, I think,
to too much.
Better to be a bird, like this one—

an ornament of the eternal.
As he came down once, to the nest of the grass,
"Squander the day, but save the soul,"
I heard him say.

Gratitude

What did you notice?

The dew-snail;
the low-flying sparrow;
the bat, on the wind, in the dark;
big-chested geese, in the V of sleekest performance;
the soft toad, patient in the hot sand;
the sweet-hungry ants;
the uproar of mice in the empty house;
the tin music of the cricket's body;
the blouse of the goldenrod.

What did you hear?

The thrush greeting the morning;
the little bluebirds in their hot box;
the salty talk of the wren,
then the deep cup of the hour of silence.

What did you admire?

The oaks, letting down their dark and hairy fruit;
the carrot, rising in its elongated waist;
the onion, sheet after sheet, curved inward to the
pale green wand;
at the end of summer the brassy dust, the almost liquid
beauty of the flowers;
then the ferns, scrawned black by the frost.

What astonished you?

The swallows making their dip and turn over the water.

What would you like to see again?

My dog: her energy and exuberance, her willingness,
 her language beyond all nimbleness of tongue, her
 recklessness, her loyalty, her sweetness, her
 strong legs, her curled black lip, her snap.

What was most tender?

Queen Anne's lace, with its parsnip root;
the everlasting in its bonnets of wool;
the kinks and turns of the tupelo's body;
the tall, blank banks of sand;
the clam, clamped down.

What was most wonderful?

The sea, and its wide shoulders;
the sea and its triangles;
the sea lying back on its long athlete's spine.

What did you think was happening?

The green breast of the hummingbird;
the eye of the pond;
the wet face of the lily;
the bright, puckered knee of the broken oak;
the red tulip of the fox's mouth;
the up-swing, the down-pour, the frayed sleeve
 of the first snow—

so the gods shake us from our sleep.

Oranges

Cut one, the lace of acid
rushes out, spills over your hands.
You lick them, manners don't come into it.
Orange—the first word you have heard that day—

enters your mind. Everybody then
does what he or she wants—breakfast is casual.
Slices, quarters, halves, or the whole hand
holding an orange ball like the morning sun

on a day of soft wind and no clouds
which it so often is. "Oh, I always
want to live like this,
flying up out of the furrows of sleep,

fresh from water and its sheer excitement,
felled as though by a miracle
at this first sharp taste of the day!"
You're shouting, but no one is surprised.

Here, there, everywhere on the earth
thousands are rising and shouting with you—
even those who are utterly silent, absorbed—
their mouths filled with such sweetness.

Moonlight

Now comes the white-striped, sharp-nosed digger of dampness
    in her black and oily coat.
All night in the moonlight she has been wandering
    the stony beach; now she steps
into the gardens and under the street lights
    like a flat cat.

Her eyes gleaming and her tail aloft, she is afraid
    of nothing—not dogs, not policemen who see her
and do not remove themselves from their cruisers, but sail on
    down the dark roads.

Everything is famous for something: the eagle for power,
    the fox for cunning.
This one we know for her temper and also her smell,
    which comes from the wicks of fire.
Yet once I watched and heard her, deep in the woods,
    humming to herself as she carried
leaves into her humble house, that was nothing
    but a scratched-out hole.

Take care you don't know anything in this world
    too quickly or easily. Everything
is also a mystery, and has its own secret aura in the moonlight,
    its private song.

           If you meet her
don't be afraid, just stand still.
And, while you let her stare you down,

notice how she stamps her pretty, little feet.
Notice how she shines.

Now Are the Rough Things Smooth

Now are the rough things smooth, and the smooth things stand in flickering slats, facing the slow tarnish of sun-fall. Summer is over, or nearly. And therefore the green is not green anymore but yellow, beige, russet, rust; all the darknesses are beginning to settle in. And therefore why pray to permanence, why not pray to impermanence, to change, to—whatever comes next. Willingness is next to godliness. Once I watched a swallow playing with a feather, high in the blue air. The swallow wanted to fly and frolic; the feather just wanted to float. Many times the swallow dropped the feather, which drifted away, then went diving and careening after it. There are so many things to do in this world, and so many things to be done. Right now I'm glad to be agile and insistent. But, later! Then, I'll be happy to give up the quick burst, oh darling and important world, and just float away.

A Settlement

Look, it's spring. And last year's loose dust has turned into this soft willingness. The wind-flowers have come up trembling, slowly the brackens are up-lifting their curvaceous and pale bodies. The thrushes have come home, none less than filled with mystery, sorrow, happiness, music, ambition.

And I am walking out into all of this with nowhere to go and no task undertaken but to turn the pages of this beautiful world over and over, in the world of my mind.

* * *

Therefore, dark past,
I'm about to do it.
I'm about to forgive you

for everything.

Their Wings

In summer the bats
fly like dots and dashes
over the evening pond

on the darkness
of their wings.
But once, in the morning,

one of them lay on the road,
struggling,
so I carried it off into the woods and laid it

in a mossy place, in an old stump, where it died
heart-thumping and hissing,
in the slump of its wings,

in the huge enfeeblement of everything,
and in what dread I don't know,
and in what panic I don't know either.

In death
it was a mad architecture—
its joints were too many; it shed

all sound, all power—became
a little heap of stiffness
with a monkey face.

At dusk the others still
whirl through the air,
content

in the fist of their bodies.
And so I see
how steep the fall for everything—

what all become
past howl and breath—how the eyes fill
with an endless void,

and the tiny rose of the tongue
grows still,
and the leaves around

don't seem to notice or care,
but lean forward, like green wings,
upon the air.

Her Grave, Again

1.

Late summer, and once again the egrets have come back.
They stand in the marsh like white flowers.
Like flowers slowly flying, they cross over the dark water.

And the palavering wind
is walking
through the pines

talking and talking—

not necessarily softly.

2. (Luke)

I suppose by now
the delicate click beetles, the dark and robust bacteria,
have gone skipping in and out of her silent house: her
    heavy, relaxed bones.

For now she is God's dog.
(The deep electric kindness of her eyes.)

For now her life is over, who never once did wrong.
(And still, in the fields,
a bird with a ruby throat is thrusting
its tongue into
the sopped lip
of the lily.)

The death went into her
like lightning
in slow motion,
it mashed her knees,
it ruined the red glove of her heart.

(God puts two fingers into his mouth. Above the long beard,
the nose hooked like a thin moon, one eye like Venus
and the other like Mars. And he whistles. And we come.)

3. *(Remembering)*

Her hum.
Her sturdy legs.
Her white teeth.
Her heart-cage.
Her dew claws.
Her eyelashes.

4.

Fabre told a thousand stories,
each one as true
as he could make it.
He looked and looked.
I do that too, so can you.
The little jumping spider has green eyes,
and here is the lid of the eye—
and here is the hair along the lid of the eye,
it's amazing!
Now, try a bird.

Look, here is the head, the horn beak, the waffle of the tongue.
Look, here is the narrow chute of the throat, color of sunrise.
And here are the toes curled on the limb in the
    valley of leaves.
Do you see it!
And then the bird, unhurried, as though filled
with a fragrance to which it must make some reply, lifts
its small, soft head, and begins

to sing.

               5. *(Remembering)*

Often
she steps down into my dream
for a visit,
she hovers
as in the old days
at my shoulder,
she sulks
until we run out together
into the world,
then she prances

through the bogs and over the dunes
then she gallops back to me
as in the old days
and leaps against me
her body

as in the old days
touching me
with the two wings of our lives,

6.

love
and terror.

7. *(Matins)*

Now we are awake
and now we are come together
and now we are thanking the Lord.

This is easy,
for the Lord is everywhere.

He is in the water and the air,
He is in the very walls.

He is around us and in us.
He is the floor on which we kneel.

We make our songs for him
as sweet as we can

for his goodness,
and, lo, he steps into the song

and out of it, having blessed it,
having recognized our intention,

having awakened us, who thought we were awake,
a second time,
having married us to the air and the water,

having lifted us in intensity,
having lowered us in beautiful amiability,

having given us
each other,
and the weeds, dogs, cities, boats, dreams
that are the world.

Blue Iris

Now that I'm free to be myself, who am I?

Can't fly, can't run, and see how slowly I walk.

Well, I think, I can read books.

                "What's that you're doing?"
the green-headed fly shouts as it buzzes past.

I close the book.

Well, I can write down words, like these, softly.

"What's that you're doing?" whispers the wind, pausing in a heap just outside the window.

Give me a little time, I say back to its staring, silver face. It doesn't happen all of a sudden, you know.

"Doesn't it?" says the wind, and breaks open, releasing distillation of blue iris.

And my heart panics not to be, as I long to be,
the empty, waiting, pure, speechless receptacle.

Walking to Oak-Head Pond, and Thinking of the Ponds I Will Visit in the Next Days and Weeks

What is so utterly invisible
as tomorrow?
Not love,
not the wind,

not the inside of a stone.
Not anything.
And yet, how often I'm fooled—
I'm wading along

in the sunlight—
and I'm sure I can see the fields and the ponds shining
days ahead—
I can see the light spilling

like a shower of meteors
into next week's trees,
and I plan to be there soon—
and, so far, I am

just that lucky,
my legs splashing
over the edge of darkness,
my heart on fire.

I don't know where
such certainty comes from—
the brave flesh
or the theater of the mind—

but if I had to guess
I would say that only
what the soul is supposed to be
could send us forth

with such cheer
as even the leaf must wear
as it unfurls
its fragrant body, and shines

against the hard possibility of stoppage
which, day after day,
before such brisk, corpuscular belief,
shudders, and gives way.

Early Snow

Amazed I looked
out of the window and saw
the early snow coming down casually,
almost drifting, over

the gardens, then the gardens began
to vanish as each white, six-pointed
snowflake lay down without a sound with all
the others. I thought, how incredible

were their numbers. I thought of dried
leaves drifting spate after spate
out of the forests,
the fallen sparrows, the hairs of all our heads,

as, still, the snowflakes went on pouring softly through
what had become dusk or anyway flung
a veil over the sun. And I thought
how not one looks like another

though each is exquisite, fanciful, and
falls without argument. It was now nearly
evening. Some crows landed and tried
to walk around then flew off. They were perhaps

laughing in crow talk or anyway so it seemed
and I might have joined in, there was something
that wonderful and refreshing
about what was by then a confident, white blanket

     carrying out its
  cheerful work, covering ruts, softening
  the earth's trials, but at the same time
there was some kind of almost sorrow that fell

     over me. It was
  the loneliness again. After all
   what is Nature, it isn't
kindness, it isn't unkindness. And I turned

and opened the door, and still the snow poured down
 smelling of iron and the pale, vast eternal, and
  there it was, whether I was ready or not:
  the silence; the blank, white, glittering sublime.

At Twilight an Angel

At twilight an angel was standing in the garden. It is true, the wings are very beautiful. Even more spectacular, in a quieter way, is the light that shines out of the angel's body. Not the cold light of the glow worm, but the softer light of a candle, or more exactly the light of a candle as it is seen through a window and, therefore, is not only itself but the light and a kind of veil together, which in fact does not double the mystery but multiplies it. The angel was looking into the trees, but mostly it was just standing there. In a strange and inexplicable way, it seemed as familiar to me as the trees themselves. I was glad it was there, but didn't expect more—I mean I didn't expect the angel to stir from its place anymore than I expected the trees to start walking around. The trees and the angel, they were each just what they were.

And yet, I am not quite telling the truth when I talk of such contentment. Once I woke in the night and was exasperated entirely, for an angel in those days, and nights too, had come into our house—had come that far—and hovered there. Why doesn't the angel help me, I thought, as I exhausted myself doing what had to be done. But the angel did not. It was, as I said, like a light behind a veil, as though Heaven's purpose could not trade itself for the business, even the grief, of the earth. Which is just one more mystery and, finally, the one I think about most. What, then, is their earnest business? What do the flames mean that spark from under their feet? Was I wrong, did the angel in the dark offer tenderness, and did I miss it? And what was that other angel doing in the garden, standing there straight-limbed and substantial, as though the trees were singing to him, or he was singing to the leaves, or all of them were stitching a music together for something or someone, and no time no precious time to think of anything else.

Snow Buntings

Nothing
all winter,
floats to our ears
more brightly

than the voices
of the sand-colored
snow buntings
that twirl from the north—

that come
tireless through the wind—
that graze
in the barest fields,

on the smallest seed,
that pour forth
their faint phrases
like flakes of water,

like bits of glaze
tapping against each other
calmly
in the white cave,

in the blue hair
of the storm.
How long is winter,
and how shall we bear it?

Day after day
they dip down
out of the clouds
and into the world

to chirr and spangle
among the rows
of corn root,
the silent snow,

until the earth is lifted
out of the great weight
of brokenness
by their clear voices

that shake
like beads of light
across the lonely fields, to make them
glow.

Winter at Herring Cove

Years ago,
in the bottle-green light
of the cold January sea,

two seals
suddenly appeared together
in a single uplifting wave—

each in exactly the same relaxed position—
each, like a large, black comma,
upright and staring;

it was like a painting
done twice
and, twice, tenderly.

The wave hung, then it broke apart;
its lip was lightning;
its floor was the blow of sand

over which the seals rose and twirled and were gone.
Of all the reasons for gladness,
what could be foremost of this one,

that the mind can seize both the instant and the memory!
Now the seals are no more than the salt of the sea.
If they live, they're more distant than Greenland.

But here's the kingdom we call remembrance
with its thousand iron doors
through which I pass so easily,

switching on the old lights as I go—
while the dead wind rises and the old rapture rewinds,
the stiff waters once more begin to kick and flow.

Tree Sparrows

I thought I heard them
in some vines
swinging down
in a yard

across the road,
so I went
this afternoon
across the white-sheeted fields,

slowly,
and listening hard,
until I found them
beside a shining creek

that was rattling
icily along—
they were foraging
the frozen buckberries

and calling out to each other
in delicate
wafers of sound.
The last time

I saw them
it was half the country away—
almost,
you might say,

in another world—
anyway, at a house
I no longer go to,
whose people

are all dead now,
whose graves, even,
I don't visit.
And the little birds

looked exactly the same!
Trim and bold,
and empty of any memory
that could break the spell

of the moment,
they flew from branch to branch;
they sang
in the great, white cold.

The Loon

    Not quite four a.m., when the rapture of being alive
    strikes me from sleep, and I rise
    from the comfortable bed and go
    to another room, where my books are lined up
    in their neat and colorful rows. How

    magical they are! I choose one
    and open it. Soon
    I have wandered in over the waves of the words
    to the temple of thought.

                        And then I hear
    outside, over the actual waves, the small,
    perfect voice of the loon. He is also awake,
    and with his heavy head uplifted he calls out
    to the fading moon, to the pink flush
    swelling in the east that, soon,
    will become the long, reasonable day.

                              Inside the house
    it is still dark, except for the pool of lamplight
    in which I am sitting.

                    I do not close the book.

    Neither, for a long while, do I read on.

Snowy Night

Last night, an owl
in the blue dark
tossed
an indeterminate number

of carefully shaped sounds into
the world, in which,
a quarter of a mile away, I happened
to be standing.

I couldn't tell
which one it was—
the barred or the great-horned
ship of the air—

it was that distant. But, anyway,
aren't there moments
that are better than knowing something,
and sweeter? Snow was falling,

so much like stars
filling the dark trees
that one could easily imagine
its reason for being was nothing more

than prettiness. I suppose
if this were someone else's story
they would have insisted on knowing
whatever is knowable—would have hurried

over the fields
to name it—the owl, I mean.
But it's mine, this poem of the night,
and I just stood there, listening and holding out

my hands to the soft glitter
falling through the air. I love this world,
but not for its answers.
And I wish good luck to the owl,

whatever its name—
and I wish great welcome to the snow,
whatever its severe and comfortless
and beautiful meaning.

Mink

A mink,
    jointless as heat, was
tip-toeing along
    the edge of the creek,

which was still in its coat of snow,
    yet singing—I could hear it!—
the old song
    of brightness.

It was one of those places,
    turning and twisty,
that Ruskin might have painted, though
    he didn't. And there were trees
leaning this way and that,
    seed-beaded

buckthorn mostly, but at the moment
    no bird, the only voice
that of the covered water—like a long,
    unknotted thread, it kept
slipping through. The mink
    had a hunger in him

bigger than his shadow, which was gathered
    like a sheet of darkness under his
neat feet which were busy
    making dents in the snow. He sniffed
slowly and thoroughly in all
    four directions, as though

it was a prayer to the whole world, as far
     as he could capture its beautiful
smells—the iron of the air, the blood
     of necessity. Maybe, for him, even
the pink sun fading away to the edge
     of the world had a smell,

of roses, or of terror, who knows
     what his keen nose was
finding out. For me, it was the gift of the winter
     to see him. Once, like a hot, dark-brown pillar,
he stood up—and then he ran forward, and was gone.
     I stood awhile and then walked on

over the white snow: the terrible, gleaming
     loneliness. It took me, I suppose,
something like six more weeks to reach
     finally a patch of green, I paused so often
to be glad, and grateful, and even then carefully across
     the vast, deep woods I kept looking back.

LONG LIFE

ESSAYS AND OTHER WRITINGS

2004

CONTENTS

Foreword / 131

PART ONE: FLOW

Flow / 135

Habits, Differences, and the Light That Abides / 141

Poem: Can You Imagine? / 145

Three Histories and a Hummingbird / 146

PART TWO: WORDSWORTH'S MOUNTAIN

Wordsworth's Mountain / 153

Dog Talk / 157

The Perfect Days / 163

Poem: Just as the Calendar Began to Say Summer / 166

Waste Land: An Elegy / 167

PART THREE: ARTISTS OF THE BEAUTIFUL

Emerson: An Introduction / 173

Hawthorne's *Mosses from an Old Manse* / 181

The House of the Seven Gables / 191

PART FOUR: DUST

Prose Poem: Are You Okay? / 203

Poem: Softest of Mornings / 204

Dust / 205

Sand Dabs, Seven / 208

Poem: The Morning Walk / 210

Sand Dabs, Eight / 211

Comfort / 213

Sand Dabs, Nine / 215

Home / 217

Poem: Summer Night / 220

Poem: Carrying the Snake to the Garden / 221

Poem: By the Wild-Haired Corn / 223

Where I Live / 224

Poem: Waking on a Summer Morning / 228

Prose Poem: One Winter Day / 229

Foreword

I WOULD RATHER write poems than prose, any day, any place. Yet each has its force. Prose flows forward bravely and, often, serenely, only slowly exposing emotion. Every character, every idea piques our interest, until the complexity of it is its asset; we begin to feel a whole culture under and behind it. Poems are less cautious, and the voice of the poem remains somehow solitary. And it is a flesh and bone voice, that slips and slides and leaps over the bank and out onto any river it meets, landing, with sharp blades, on the smallest piece of ice. Working on prose and working on poems elicit different paces from the heartbeat. One is nicer to feel than the other, guess which one. When I have spent a long time with prose I feel the weight of the work. But when I work at poems, the word is in error; it isn't like any other labor. Poems either do not succeed, or they feel as much delivered as created.

Still, the endeavors of narrative, or the amble of description toward thought, have their enchantments. And there are so many moods of prose—the explanation, the exhortation, the moral instruction, the comedy. And do not forget the fantastical story made buoyant with glitter and the shadows of glitter, too small and sweet, perhaps, for any other use.

We talk about poems turning the line—that magical device—but of course prose turns, too, where the paper is about to run out. Such steadiness! But the prose-horse is in harness, a good, sturdy and comfortable harness, while the horse of poetry has wings. And I would rather fly than plow.

I have written two books about writing poetry, and this is not another one. I hoped to shun that subject altogether. I have failed, but only very briefly and I hope in a sporting manner. In time I will keep silence altogether. Poets must read and study, but also they must learn to tilt and whisper, shout, or dance, each in his or her own way, or we might just as well copy the old books. But, no, that would never do, for always the new self swimming around in the old world feels itself uniquely verbal. And that is just the point: how the world, moist and bountiful, calls to each of us to make a new and serious response. That's the big question, the one the world throws at you every morning. "Here you are, alive. Would you like to make a comment?" This book is my comment.

One more thing I want to mention before the pages actually begin. Writing poems, for me but not necessarily for others, is a way of offering praise to the world. In this book you will find, set among the prose pieces, a few poems. Think of them that way, as little alleluias. They're not trying to explain anything, as the prose does. They just sit there on the page, and breathe. A few lilies, or wrens, or trout among the mysterious shadows, the cold water, and the somber oaks.

PART ONE
FLOW

Flow

WE LIVE, M. and I, about ten feet from the water. When there is a storm and the wind pushes toward us from the southeast we live about a foot from the water. It sings all day long and all night as well, never the same music. Wind, temperature, where the tide is, how the moon is tugging or shoving—each of these makes a difference. The tide going out sounds harsher than the voice of its rising, what seems like a disinclination to leave growls in it, with the sound of dark, thick-stringed instruments. Coming in, it is more playful. Every day my early morning walk along the water grants me a second waking. My feet are nimble, now my ears wake, and give thanks for the ocean's song.

This enormity, this cauldron of changing greens and blues, is the great palace of the earth. Everything is in it—monsters, devils, jewels, swimming angels, soft-eyed mammals that unhesitatingly exchange looks with us as we stand on the shore; also, sunk with some ship or during off-loading, artifacts of past decades or centuries; also the outpourings of fire under water, the lava trails; and kelp fields, coral shelves, and so many other secrets—the remembered and faithfully repeated recitations of the whales, the language of dolphins—and the multitude itself, the numbers and the kinds of shark, seal, worm, vegetations, and fish: cod, haddock, swordfish, hake, also the lavender sculpin, the chisel-mouth, the goldeye, the puffer, the tripletail, the stargazing minnow. How can we not know that, already, we live in paradise?

~

But even paradise must have rules. I do not know whether or not these rules were engendered in the beginning by divine deftness or by chance. I rather think chance was the origin—though perhaps the chance was offered divinely—for the rules are neither nice nor neat; simply workable, and therefore, in the quest for life rather than no-life, sublime. Every vitality must have a mechanism that recommends it to existence—what seems like ornamentation or phantasm is pure utility. It comes from an engine of mist and electricity that may be playful, and must be assertive. And also, against the odds of endurance in the great-shouldered sea, prolific.

~

On a July morning, after a moon tide, I walk along the water's edge. In the night, thousands of small fish have been caught on the sand. Some, in the morning light, are already hot and have lost the body's capacity to move; others are still flickering, or grinding into the wet sand, or trying, with snapping motions, to move back down the swash. But it is their last hour. It is as if the ocean were spraying forth, purging itself, which certainly it is not. The fish have simply been stranded, by their proximity to shore and the unusually high tide. The sand lance has neither length nor heft, most are no more than three or four inches long. Others, not too many, are perhaps six or seven inches from face to tail. Now, in their slippery huddle, they compose an unbroken rope at the edge of the water. At places this rope is half a foot high.

Each fish has an olive-green, silvery, daintily freckled body; what is known as a superior mouth, with the lower jaw extending past the upper jaw; a pale belly; a caudal fin. The eyes are the phantasms, with their glare and their circularity. In death the jaw hangs open. The tongue is pink in the pinch of the mouth, the throat is a narrow, translucent chute. As the hour grows warmer, blood-color gathers at the gills, the skin stiffens. And still there are some shimmying and bucking a few inches toward the receding water. But none gets back. The mischief of the tides has them.

Now, a young man coming down the beach fills a plastic bag with the lances, for bait. He gathers both the trembling and the inert. Even dead this pretty little fish can catch another fish—maybe a big fish.

The next morning I go back; the beach is pale, shining, and absolutely clean.

—

But even as the multitude attracts our attention, so does the single creature and moment. I am walking with my dogs along the beach at a low and still lowering tide, when a thrashing in the shallows catches my eye. I wade to it; in the water that is little more than ankle deep, there is a stranded goosefish. Such a grotesque body, such a funeral of a mouth, the widest gate to darkness, for the size of the whole fish, that you could ever imagine! Most of the goosefish, in fact, is mouth. But also how glorious a color is each green eye—more vitally green than emeralds, than wet moss, than the leaves of violets, and shining, very much alive. I did not know what to do. One could not pick up that spiny and toothy body. Then a man came walking along with two children. They waded out and looked at the unhappy fish. He asked me for my dog's leash, which was hanging around my shoulders, and he looped it lightly under the heavy body and with the slightest tug drew the fish up, just inches, and slowly, as with a fantastic, footless dog, he led it into deeper water. Hurrah for that man's inventive mind and good heart! The fish, with the great mouth gaping, and the green eyes opening and closing, wallowed along until it could set itself down into the water entirely. Then it slipped neatly from the loop of the leash, and was gone.

—

Now it's March, the bluebirds are skating the air. Now it's April, and the whales have come home. The finbacks and the humpbacks and the rare right whales, arriving along the coast, coming into the bay, sometimes into the harbor, their massive length and weight churning and breaching as though they, like us, know playfulness. *He maketh the deep to boil like a pot, he maketh a path to shine after him,* said Job, who, I fear, could not know that there is also a reasoning and a gentleness in these mountains of flesh. Once a whale tangled in line came into the harbor with another swimming just alongside, a companion that would not leave the roped animal but lingered, while brave men went out in little boats and were able to cut the entangling line away. The eye of the humpback is like all the darkness and hope and pain one sees in the eye of the elephant, in whose brain, it is avowed by those who know, nothing is ever forgotten. It is an eye deeper than the deepest well. Once on a late spring day M. and I were standing on a boat deck when a humpback breached—leaped out of the water beside us—and trumpeted. Mist fountained from the blowhole, light flung a rainbow through the moisture; softly the mist rose and rained down onto the deck and baptized all of us.

—

One finds their bones sometimes, old and porous, come ashore years ago and, caught in the rock groins jutting out from the land, growing smaller, then smaller, decade by decade. Here, too, other interesting things are uncovered. Some of these are manmade: bits of broken dishes, nails and bolts swollen into thumbs of iron flake, old fishing lures. Here also lie many broken and empty shells, the most common those of the several kinds of clams that live in these sands; also, scallops, whelks, oysters. And there is the ice-cream-cone worm—or, at least, and especially after the somewhat but not altogether rock-tempered turbulence of storm, its empty habitation. This is an excellent fortification in the usual weathers—an elongated funnel perhaps four inches long but sometimes less, that the worm builds into the sand and of it, yet separate from it. Here it lives, upside-down, with its feathery head just able to emerge under the water and feel around. It can slip up and out a little also, then return entirely and snugly into its strange cabin. The cone, or funnel, is made of grains of sand glued together with a saliva produced by the worm for this purpose. The cone is nearly weightless and grows more so as it dries out. Its seamless wall is translucent, flecked with specks of color according to the grains of sand gathered: some light, some black, with much variety between. The grains are of a remarkably similar size; the worm can make so judicious a selection.

After a while those I bring home disassemble, by themselves or some smallest accidental tap. Then what is there but a thimbleful of sand the color of old muslin? The arrangement was all, and the energy that made the arrangement. Still, each is part of the world. I take them back to the edge of the water, to the earthpile of ever reusable materials.

―

Seven of us, and one dog, are aboard the boat. It has a single wide sail. Built years ago by the parents of our young captain, after the manner of the Bahama dinghy, it is a workboat, fairly wide, with a deep keel—a lovely creation if there ever was one. Josiah sits with the lines in his hands. He seems to be in a kind of friendly correspondence with the sail and the wind.

So we become, for the afternoon, sea creatures ourselves. How light our bodies feel as we lounge against the planks and trail our hands in the water. Ahead is the sandy point of our destination, and between us and it not a single apportioning marker but the wide water's drowsy lap and slide, its abundance and gleam. We stroll on its surface freely, citizens of the water world. How different from the foot on the stone, the hand opening the gate, the gravel path of the garden, the trudge through loose sand, the heel sticking into the clay of the field! Such weight, on the earth, is on our shoulders: gravity keeping us at home. But on the water we shake off the harness of weight; we glide; we are passengers of a sleek ocean bird with its single white wing filled with wind.

At the sandy point, Josiah throws out the anchor. Some of us swim. Some of us sit and stare through the afternoon light. Then, slowly, we come home, joking, laughing, and silent too. Once a loon breaks from the water, it runs for a long while upon the surface before the noble body can rise. Shearwaters and petrels fly around us; clouds, passing by, darken patches of the water as they hurry to their tasks in the distance.

All through our gliding journey, on this day as on so many others, a little song runs through my mind. I say a song because it passes musically, but it is really just words, a thought that is neither strange nor complex. In fact, how strange it would be *not* to think it—not to have such music inside one's head and body, on such an afternoon. What does it mean, say the words, that the earth is so beautiful? And what shall I do about it? What is the gift that I should bring to the world? What is the life that I should live?

Habits, Differences, and the Light That Abides

1.

IN THE SHAPELINESS of a life, habit plays its sovereign role. The religious literally wear it. Most people take action by habit in small things more often than in important things, for it's the simple matters that get done readily, while the more somber and interesting, taking more effort and being more complex, often must wait for another day. Thus, we could improve ourselves quite well by habit, by its judicious assistance, but it's more likely that habits rule us.

The bird in the forest or the fox on the hill has no such opportunity to forgo the important for the trivial. Habit, for these, is also the garment they wear, and indeed the very structure of their body life. It's now or never for all their vitalities—bonding, nest building, raising a family, migrating or putting on the deeper coat of winter—all is done on time and with devoted care, even if events contain also playfulness, grace, and humor, those inseparable spirits of vitality. Neither does the tree hold back its leaves but lets them flow open or glide away when the time is right. Neither does water make its own decision about freezing or not; that moment rests with the rule of temperatures.

Men and women of faith who pray—that is, who come to a certain assigned place, at definite times, and are not abashed to go down on their knees—will not tarry for the cup of coffee or the newsbreak or the end of the movie when the moment arrives. The habit, then, has become their life. What some might call the restrictions of the daily office they find to be an opportunity to foster the inner life. The hours are appointed and named; they are the Lord's. Life's fretfulness is transcended. The different and the novel are sweet, but regularity and repetition are also teachers. Divine attentiveness cannot be kept casually, or visited only in season, like Venice or Switzerland. Or, perhaps it can, but then how attentive is it? And if you have no ceremony, no habits, which may be opulent or may be simple but are exact and rigorous and familiar, how can you reach toward the actuality of faith, or even a moral life, except vaguely? The patterns of our lives reveal us. Our habits measure us. Our battles with our habits speak of dreams yet to become real. I would like to be like the fox, earnest in devotion and humor both, or the brave, compliant pond shutting its heavy door for the long winter. But, not yet have I reached that bright life or that white happiness—not yet.

2.

M. and I have plagued each other with our differences for more than forty years. But it is also a tonic. M. will hardly look at a bush. She wants a speedboat; I want to sit down on the sand and look around and get dreamy; I want to see what spirits are peeking out of the faces of the roses. Years ago M. took flying lessons. In the afternoons I got to stand at the edge of the harbor and watch her stall the small plane over the water. That means you cut the engine and let the plane drop, nose first, down. Then you start the engine again, while the plane is dropping, and you level it, hopefully, and swoop away. Week after week M. came home looking the way I feel when I've seen wild swans. It was terrifying, and wonderful.

Along with the differences that abide in each of us, there is also in each of us the maverick, the darling stubborn one who won't listen, who insists, who chooses preference or the spirited guess over yardsticks or even history. I suspect this maverick is somewhat what the soul is, or at least that the soul lives close by and companionably with its agitating and inquiring force. And of course all of it, the differences and the maverick uprisings, are part of the richness of life. If you are too much like myself, what shall I learn of you, or you of me? I bring home sassafras leaves and M. looks and admires. She tells me how it feels to float in the air above the town and the harbor, and my world is sweetened by her description of those blue miles. The touch of our separate excitements is another of the gifts of our life together.

3.

I read Jacob Boehme and am caught in his shining web. Here are Desire and Will that should be (he says) as two arms at one task; in my life they are less cooperative. Will keeps sliding away down the hill, to play when work is called for, and Desire piously wants to labor when the best season of merriment is around me. Troublemakers, both of them. And as for Boehme's third ingredient, that one remains the luminous shadow. I think it is called grace, in my language; and in my days the trail grows warm often, but the flame of it is still somewhere else. Nevertheless, I believe, with William James, that the religious life, however it is perceived and followed, is, as he wrote, "mankind's most important function." It is my Desire, thoroughly so. It is my Will, too, when I recall it from its dancing in the field, loathe to go into the schoolhouse.

But, anyway, I make little use of the schoolhouse; it is the natural world that has always offered the hint of our single and immense divinity—a million unopened fountains. In such a mood then, not of understanding but of knowing I am blessed even as moving from shade to sunlight we feel the engendering heat, I live my life. I walk along every path, or maybe I lie down at the edge of the pond to do a little summing up. Once in the early morning, I came upon a tree that was covered as if in limpid leaves, but they weren't leaves, they were butterflies—monarchs—thousands of them asleep, creating for a night and morning a single tree of orange silks, small patches of orange silks. Once I looked across a hillside and saw three deer, lying down, and a flock of geese moving among them, stepping over their legs, casually brushing against their shoulders as they pulled at the pale winter grass. Once I saw the freshly built dam of two beaver, a half moon of mud and slender branches, the leaves still fresh upon them; then, as I watched, the water shoved with its silver gloves and it broke, it left the world forever. Hurry, hurry, open every door! says my heart. The black ants, running up and down their organized hill, are an opportunity. The soft toad in the hot sand is an opportunity. One hour at the edge of the waving sea is a feast of opportunities. Every morning, tumult and quietude marry each other and create light. The sun rises like a rosy plum. Birds, floating in the water, turn to watch. Sometimes, also, or so it seems, does the wind.

Poem: Can You Imagine?

For example, what the trees do
not only in lightning storms
or the watery dark of a summer night
or under the white nets of winter
but now, and now, and now—whenever
we're not looking. Surely you can't imagine
they just stand there looking the way they look
when we're looking; surely you can't imagine
they don't dance, from the root up, wishing
to travel a little, not cramped so much as wanting
a better view, or more sun, or just as avidly
more shade—surely you can't imagine they just
stand there loving every
minute of it, the birds or the emptiness, the dark rings
of the years slowly and without a sound
thickening, and nothing different unless the wind,
and then only in its own mood, comes
to visit, surely you can't imagine
patience, and happiness, like that.

Three Histories and a Hummingbird

1.

We went together into the woods to visit the dear graves, and could not find them. We walked down the familiar wood road, but with difficulty. Tree branches and even entire trees had fallen and nothing had been cleared away. The road became a path, as it always had, then the path became uncertain. The trees, mostly birch and pine and oak, had grown so very large since we had last seen them.

It was April, a mourning cloak sailed by, and a blueheaded vireo sang high in a tree, not for us but we could think so if we wanted to. So we did that. But the graves we could not find.

2.

Judith Jefferson, sister of the father of the president, married George Farrar; they had a son named William, whose daughter, Judith, married a man named John Bowdoin.

Their daughter, Mary, married Vincent Allen, whose son Turner Allen moved to North Carolina and married Martha Montgomery, about whom we know only a little; she died young.

Their oldest son, William Vincent, married Ella Jones—we are now in the time of the War Between the States. Ella was perhaps Welsh, something not entirely known, in any case her father was Dr. John Hughes Jones, and there was little more to his story after the stormy night he caught pneumonia, traveling back from a sick man's farmhouse. Holy, holy, holy are the better labors of men. Ella Jones and William Vincent Allen had three sons; the youngest, Samuel, married Mollie Reinacher, not in the South but in California. Their oldest daughter, Ruth—now we are in the twentieth century—married Frederick J. Cook of San Francisco. And their daughter is Molly Malone Cook, who is the Whistler.

3.

I had an aunt named Agnes, this is what I know about her. Agnes means lamb, the gentle animal, therefore she was inaptly named. She was the youngest of three sisters, and perhaps spoiled. Once, in the city where she was born, she walked down the main street at the head of a parade, hand in hand with Buffalo Bill.

All the applause indicated, finally, nothing. She married a man whose hands could not cease from their small expressions of anguish; they shook always. He killed himself the unspectacular way, sluicing the exhaust of his car back into its interior. For a few years my aunt kept to her room. Later she began to go out into the night, with escorts, more than one. Which also came to nothing.

Finally I think she hated everything and then there was nothing left but the birds. She fed them extravagantly until the neighbors complained that the pigeons were wasting away the shingles of their houses. Also she fed homeless cats, but then they proliferated and she demanded they be shot.

This is the way she went on, holy, holy, holy, spending her life, feeding birds and being mean, until both, I think, were habits she could not break. Her sting raised welts in all our hearts.

Little by little the house grew empty; my grandfather died, my father, my grandmother, then my mother, and then she was alone. She moved to an apartment not far away; someone told me once that she was seen often on the sidewalk and curb, with bags of birdseed which she scattered about. I did nothing, God forgive me. A few years later a cousin sent me a postcard. It read, "Your aunt died, I thought you would want to know." He did not say which aunt, but in any case it is over now surely. When I was a little girl my grandmother used to pick bouquets of flowers from our gardens and take them to the graves, every Sunday. She never missed. That was the old way. Which has vanished now. No one goes to the graves. It was a Sunday dream. It was a dream.

4.

What can we do about God, who makes and then breaks every god-forsaken, beautiful day?

What can we do about all those graves
in the woods, in old pastures in small towns in the bellies of cities?

God's heavy footsteps through the bracken through the bog through the dark wood his breath like a swollen river

his switch, lopping the flowers, forgive me, Lord, how I

still, sometimes,
crave understanding.

5.

Down the road I went, in the morning, to see if the hummingbird was on his branch—to feel, if he was not, the little ping of his absence. Time was, he was there almost every day, swinging his head like a green jewel above the larkspur and the lilies. Then the rains came, then the fall, then the white sheet of the winter, and I waited. But he has not come back again, not ever, not yet.

PART TWO

WORDSWORTH'S MOUNTAIN

Wordsworth's Mountain

1.

THERE IS A RUMOR of total welcome among the frosts of the winter morning. Beauty has its purposes, which, all our lives and at every season, it is our opportunity, and our joy, to divine. Nothing outside ourselves makes us desire to do so; the questions, and the striving toward answers, come from within. The field I am looking at is perhaps twenty acres altogether, long and broad. The sun has not yet risen but is sending its first showers over the mountains, a kind of rehearsal, a slant light with even a golden cast. I do not exaggerate. The light touches every blade of frozen grass, which then burns as a particular as well as part of the general view. The still upright weeds have become wands, encased in a temporary shirt of ice and light. Neither does this first light miss the opportunity of the small pond, or the groups of pine trees. And now: enough of silver, behold the pink, even a vague, unsurpassable flush of pale green. It is the performance of this hour only, the dawning of the day, fresh and ever new. This is to say nothing against afternoons evenings or even midnight. Each has its portion of the spectacular. But dawn—dawn is a gift. Much is revealed about a person by his or her passion, or indifference, to this opening of the door of day. No one who loves dawn, and is abroad to see it, could be a stranger to me.

Poe claimed he could hear the night darkness as it poured, in the evening, into the world. I remember this now and think, reversing the hour but not the idea, that I will hear some sound of the morning as it settles upward. What I hear, though, is no such sprawling and powerful anthem, as it would have to be, but the rustling of a flock of snow buntings, high and wild in the cold air, like seeds, rushing toward me, and then away. Seeds that sing. I see, on this morning, nothing else, or nothing else moving. Fox tracks are ahead of mine, dimpling the frost, but the fox is nowhere in view.

2.

When I was a child, living in a small town surrounded by woods and a winding creek—woods more pastoral than truly wild—my great pleasure, and my secret, was to fashion for myself a number of little houses. They were huts really, made of sticks and grass, maybe a small heap of fresh leaves inside. There was never a closure but always an open doorway, and I would sit just inside, looking out into the world. Such architectures were the capsules of safety, and freedom as well, open to the wind, made of grass and smelling like leaves and flowers. I was lucky, no one ever found any of my houses, or harmed them. They fell apart of the weather, an event that caused me no grief; I moved on to another place of leaves and earth, and built anew.

Many children build in this way, but more often than not as a social act, where they play the games of territory and society. For me it was important to be alone; solitude was a prerequisite to being openly and joyfully susceptible and responsive to the world of leaves, light, birdsong, flowers, flowing water. Most of the adult world spoke of such things as opportunities, and materials. To the young these materials are still celestial; for every child the garden is recreated. Then the occlusions begin. The mountain and the forest are sublime but the valley soil raises richer crops. The perfect gift is no longer a single house but a house, or a mind, divided. Man finds he has two halves to his existence: leisure and occupation, and from these separate considerations he now looks upon the world. In leisure he remembers radiance; in labor he looks for results.

But in those early years I did not think about such things. I simply went out into the green world and made my house, a kind of cowl, or a dream, or a palace of grass.

3.

And now I am thinking of the poet Wordsworth, and the strange adventure that one night overtook him. When he was still a young boy, in love with summer and night, he went down to a lake, "borrowed" a rowboat, and rowed out upon the water. At first he felt himself embraced by pleasures: the moonlight, the sound of the oars in the calm water. Then, suddenly, a mountain peak nearby, with which he was familiar, or *felt* he was familiar, revealed, to his mind and eye, a horrifying flexibility. All crag and weight, it *perceived* him; it leaned down over the water; it seemed to pursue him. Of course he was terrified, and rowed hard, fleeing back across the water. But the experience led him, led his mind, from simple devotion of that beauty which is a harmony, a kindly ministry of thought, to nature's deeper and inexplicable greatness. The gleam and the tranquility of the natural world he loved always, and now he honored also the world's brawn and mystery, its machinations that lie beyond our understanding—that are not even nameable. What Wordsworth praised thereafter was more than the arrangement of concretions and vapors into appreciable and balanced landscapes; it was, also, the whirlwind. The beauty and strangeness of the world may fill the eyes with its cordial refreshment. Equally it may offer the heart a dish of terror. On one side is radiance; on another is the abyss.

4.

Wordsworth, though he did not think so on that summer evening, was a lucky boy. I, in my hut of leaves, was a lucky girl. Something touched, between us and the universe. It does not always happen. But if it does, we know forever where we live, no matter where we sleep, or eat our dinner, or sit at table and write words on paper.

And we might, in our lives, have many thresholds, many houses to walk out from and view the stars, or to turn and go back to for warmth and company. But the real one—the actual house not of beams and nails but of existence itself—is all of earth, with no door, no address separate from oceans or stars, or from pleasure or wretchedness either, or hope, or weakness, or greed.

How wonderful that the universe is beautiful in so many places and in so many ways. But also the universe is brisk and businesslike, and no doubt does not give its delicate landscapes or its thunderous displays of power, and perhaps perception, too, for our sakes or our improvement. Nevertheless, its intonations are our best tonics, if we would take them. For the universe is full of radiant suggestion. For whatever reason, the heart cannot separate the world's appearance and actions from morality and valor, and the power of every idea is intensified, if not actually created, by its expression in substance. Over and over in the butterfly we see the idea of transcendence. In the forest we see not the inert but the aspiring. In water that departs forever and forever returns, we experience eternity.

Dog Talk

HE IS AHEAD OF ME in the fields, poking about in the grass. By the time I reach him the last of the newborn field mice are disappearing down his throat. His eyes roll upward to read my mood—praise, amusement or disapproval—but I only touch his head casually and walk on. Let him make his own judgment. The mice construct thick, cupped nests deep in the grass from which they travel along a multitude of tunneled paths—to the creek perhaps, or into the orchard to find a bruised apple or a leaf of mint, or buckberries. Then they hurry home again, to the peep and swirl of their nestlings. But these babes have been crunched on Ben's molars, have begun the descent through darkness and acids toward transformation. I hope they were well crunched.

At home Ben "wolfs" his food, as the saying goes. He barely lifts his face from the bowl, scarcely breathes until all is gone. He came to us a lost dog, down from the Blue Ridge, and certainly he had known trouble and probably, at least for a while, hunger. He came with a split tongue, a wound mysterious and long healed, made perhaps on a roughly opened can, or by another dog during trough feeding. It is one of the secrets we will never know. The rip is an inch long, at the front of the tongue, not quite centered. Now the tongue brims forward on its final slide in two directions, or hangs to both sides of his right fang tooth, which stands above the mossy bulk of the tongue like a white bird on a pink sea.

Other quirks and mannerisms, frights and anxieties, Ben brought with him, and has kept. Mostly he wants reasonable things—quiet, security, both M. and me within sight. He is frightened of lightning, brooms, kindling, backfire, and trucks generally. He loves fields, freedom, rabbit-smell, rides in the car, lots of food. I think he can drink a gallon of water at a single stint. I think he can run for eight hours without halt. Or, he used to.

> Where's Ben?
> Down in the creek, getting muddy.

> Where's Ben?
> Out in the field eating mice again.

> Where's Ben?
> Upstairs in his bedroom sleeping on his four
> pillows and his blue blanket.

―

Of night and the dog: you cannot elaborate the dark thickness of it as he can, you cannot separate the rich, rank threads as they make their way through the grasses: mouse, vole, mink, nails of the fox then the thin stream of his urine, drops sticking to the grass blades, necklace of pale gold. And the rabbit—his paw smell, his juice or a single strand of fur, or a bleat from a gland under the white tail, or a bead of excrement, black pearls dropped off here and there. I have seen Ben place his nose meticulously into the shallow dampness of a deer's hoofprint and shut his eyes as if listening. But it is smell he is listening to. The wild, high music of smell, that we know so little about.

Tonight Ben charges up the yard; Bear follows. They run into the field and are gone. A soft wind, like a belt of silk, wraps the house.

I follow them to the end of the field where I hear the long-eared owl, at wood's edge, in one of the tall pines. All night the owl will sit there inventing his catty racket, except when he opens pale wings and drifts moth-like over the grass. I have seen both dogs look up as the bird floats by, and I suppose the field mouse hears it too, in the pebble of his tiny heart. Though I hear nothing.

—

Bear is small and white with a curly tail. He was meant to be idle and pretty but learned instead to love the world, and to romp roughly with the big dogs. The brotherliness of the two, Ben and Bear, increases with each year. They have their separate habits, their own favorite sleeping places, for example, yet each worries without letup if the other is missing. They both bark rapturously and in support of each other. They both sneeze to express pleasure, and yawn in humorous admittance of embarrassment. In the car, when we are getting close to home and the smell of the ocean begins to surround them, they both sit bolt upright and hum.

> With what vigor
> and intention to please himself
> the little white dog
> flings himself into every puddle
> on the muddy road.

—

Some things are unchangeably wild, others are stolidly tame. The tiger is wild, and the coyote, and the owl. I am tame, you are tame. There are wild things that have been altered, but only into a semblance of tameness, it is no real change. But the dog lives in both worlds. Ben is devoted, he hates the door between us, is afraid of separation. But he had, for a number of years, a dog friend to whom he was also loyal. Every day they and a few others gathered into a noisy gang, and some of their games were bloody. Dog is docile, and then forgets. Dog promises then forgets. Voices call him. Wolf faces appear in dreams. He finds himself running over incredible lush or barren stretches of land, nothing any of us has ever seen. Deep in the dream, his paws twitch, his lip lifts. The dreaming dog leaps through the underbrush, enters the earth through a narrow tunnel, and is home. The dog wakes and the disturbance in his eyes when you say his name is a recognizable cloud. How glad he is to see you, and he sneezes a little to tell you so.

But ah! the falling-back, fading dream where he was almost *there* again, in the pure, rocky, weather-ruled beginning. Where he was almost wild again and knew nothing else but that life, no other possibility. A world of trees and dogs and the white moon, the nest, the breast, the heart-warming milk! The thick-mantled ferocity at the end of the tunnel, known as father, a warrior he himself would grow to be.

Dog promises and then forgets, blame him not. The tooth glitters in the ridged mouth. The fur lifts along the spine. He lifts a leg and sprays a radiant mist over a stone, or a dead toad, or somebody's hat. He understands what is wanted, and tries, and tries again, and is good for a long time, and then forgets.

―

And it is exceedingly short, his galloping life. Dogs die so soon. I have my stories of that grief, no doubt many of you do also. It is almost a failure of will, a failure of love, to let them grow old— or so it feels. We would do anything to keep them with us, and to keep them young. The one gift we cannot give.

The Summer Beach

Baba, Chico, Obediah, Phoebe, Abigail, Emily, Emma, Josie, Pushpa, Chester, Zara, Lucky, Benjamin, Bear, Henry, Atisha, Ollie, Beulah, Gussie, Cody, Angelina, Lightning, Holly, Suki, Buster, Bazougey, Tyler, Milo, Magic, Taffy, Buffy, Thumper, Katie, Petey; Bennie, Edie, Max, Luke, Jessie, Keesha, Jasper, Brick, Briar Rose.

Bear lifts his head and listens brightly. He growls in excitement and runs to the window to look. Is it a trick or a gift, my saying aloud the names of the dogs without producing the dogs? All winter he will hurry to listen to this puzzle, this strange and wonderful pleasure.

―

But I want to extol not the sweetness nor the placidity of the dog, but the wilderness out of which he cannot step entirely, and from which we benefit. For wilderness is our first home too, and in our wild ride into modernity with all its concerns and problems we need also all the good attachments to that origin that we can keep or restore. Dog is one of the messengers of that rich and still magical first world. The dog would remind us of the pleasures of the body with its graceful physicality, and the acuity and rapture of the senses, and the beauty of forest and ocean and rain and our own breath. There is not a dog that romps and runs but we learn from him.

The other dog—the one that all its life walks leashed and obedient down the sidewalk—is what a chair is to a tree. It is a possession only, the ornament of a human life. Such dogs can remind us of nothing large or noble or mysterious or lost. They cannot make us sweeter or more kind.

Only unleashed dogs can do that. They are a kind of poetry themselves when they are devoted not only to us but to the wet night, to the moon and the rabbit-smell in the grass and their own bodies leaping forward.

―

Thunder that is still too far away for us to hear presses down on Ben's ears and he wakes us and leans hot and chesty first against M., then against me, and listens to our slow, warm words that mean we love him. But when the storm has passed, he is brave again and wants to go out. We open the door and he glides away without a backward glance. It is early, in the blue and grainy air we can just see him running along the edge of the water, into the first pink suggestion of sunrise. And we are caught by the old affinity, a joyfulness—his great and seemly pleasure in the physical world. Because of the dog's joyfulness, our own is increased. It is no small gift. It is not the least reason why we should honor as well as love the dog of our own life, and the dog down the street, and all the dogs not yet born. What would the world be like without music or rivers or the green and tender grass? What would this world be like without dogs?

The Perfect Days

A MOUNTAIN IS a mountain; on every sunny summer day it is exceedingly the same. A forest in fall, on one long blue day after another, is the same, and so it may be said for a lake, and even the oceans, whose energies run in habits that are discoverable and reliable. Ah, what a simple place then is the granular and leafy and liquid world! Except for that old master of motion, Aeolus, who keeps the winds in his cave, allowing them out only at his whim or command, to glide over the world and thus to make it not one world but a thousand—a thousand thousand! Somewhere in the past the word we use—"weather"—shaped itself out of the word meaning wind, or air. Who comes, the whisperer or the howler—the trampler, or the tender fingers of spring? It is the node of change among the fair certainties—the catalyst that can shake out our hours from quietude to rampage, or back again to beatitude.

I prefer weather in the smallest quantities. A drop will do. The best weather, it might be said, is no weather. Like the poet Wordsworth, who preferred lakes to seacoasts, and moderate and green mountains to rugged, snowcapped peaks, and long, easy walks during which one might reflect, or even be creative, to the exertions that make history, I like best weather's small, beneficent motions. They are not the sublime motions. Storm, cyclone, flood, ice and avalanche make news, and often have need of heroes. But they do not make poems. True, Shelley wrote much about Mont Blanc, its terrifying scenery and continually rearranging and polishing winds. But he himself was at a safe distance; he kept his pen wet and his paper dry and his wits focused on—thought. Excitement has its advocates, but I have never regretted missing the Bennington tornado of two or three summers ago, when the sky turned a lurid green (so it has been reported), and the trees fell like ranks of soldiers in the woods and across the roads.

The problem is, one wants, both in life and in writing, a story. And the ferocious weathers are the perfect foundation; in all tempests we must *do* something. We must *get* somewhere—and so the story begins. Truly, the heart delights in it. Adversity, even tragedy, is cathartic, and a teacher. Challenge and personal valor are admired by us all. On the windless days, when the maples have put forth their deep canopies, and the sky is wearing its new blue immensities, and the wind has dusted itself not an hour ago in some spicy field and hardly touches us as it passes by, what is it we do? We lie down and rest upon the generous earth. Very likely we fall asleep.

—

Once, years ago, I emerged from the woods in the early morning at the end of a walk and—it was the most casual of moments—as I stepped from under the trees into the mild, pouring-down sunlight I experienced a sudden impact, a *seizure* of happiness. It was not the drowning sort of happiness, rather the floating sort. I made no struggle toward it; it was given. Time seemed to vanish. Urgency vanished. Any important difference between myself and all other things vanished. I knew that I belonged to the world, and felt comfortably my own containment in the totality. I did not feel that I understood any mystery, not at all; rather that I could be happy and feel blessed within the perplexity—the summer morning, its gentleness, the sense of the great work being done though the grass where I stood scarcely trembled. As I say, it was the most casual of moments, not mystical as the word is usually meant, for there was no vision, or anything extraordinary at all, but only a sudden awareness of the citizenry of all things within one world: leaves, dust, thrushes and finches, men and women. And yet it was a moment I have never forgotten, and upon which I have based many decisions in the years since.

My story contains neither a mountain, nor a canyon, nor a blizzard, nor hail, nor spike of wind striking the earth and lifting whatever is in its path. I think the rare and wonderful awareness I felt would not have arrived in any such busy hour. Most stories about weather are swift to describe meeting the face of the storm and the argument of the air, climbing the narrow and icy trail, crossing the half-frozen swamp. I would not make such stories less by obtaining anything special for the other side of the issue. Nor would I suggest that a meeting of individual spirit and universe is impossible within the harrowing blast. Yet I would hazard this guess, that it is more likely to happen to someone attentively entering the quiet moment, when the sun-soaked world is gliding on under the blessings of blue sky, and the wind god is asleep. Then, if ever, we may peek under the veil of all appearances and partialities. We may be touched by the most powerful of suppositions—even to a certainty—as we stand in the rose petals of the sun and hear a murmur from the wind no louder than the sound it makes as it dozes under the bee's wings. This, too, I suggest, is weather, and worthy of report.

Poem: Just as the Calendar Began to Say Summer

I went out of the schoolhouse fast
and through the gardens and to the woods,
and spent all summer forgetting what I'd been taught—

two times two, and diligence, and so forth,
how to be modest and useful, and how to succeed and so forth,
machines and oil and plastic and money and so forth.

By fall I had healed somewhat, but was summoned back
to the chalky rooms and the desks, to sit and remember

the way the river kept rolling its pebbles,
the way the wild wrens sang though they hadn't a penny in the
 bank,
the way the flowers were dressed in nothing but light.

Waste Land: An Elegy

AT OUR TOWN's old burn dump, not officially used for years, discarded peppermint and raspberries reconnected their roots to the gravelly earth and went on growing; a couple of apple trees blossomed and bore each year a bushel of green and bumpy fruit. Blackberries drifted up and down the slopes; thistles, Bouncing Bet, everlasting, goldenrod, wild carrot lifted their leaves and then their flowers and then their rafts of seeds. Honeysuckle, in uplifted waves, washed toward some pink roses, no longer a neat and civilized hedge but a thorny ledge, with darkness at its hem. Now the burn dump is no more. The old world had its necessities; presently there are new ones, and they are not so simply met—nor will the old parcels of land suffice. On these few acres of land, and more, will be established the heartland of our town's sewage, where the buried pipes will converge with the waste of our lives. What a sad hilarity! I want to talk about flowers, but the necessity has become, for our visitor-rich town, how to deal with the daily sewage of, it may be, sixty thousand souls. At least that was a weekend estimate a few years ago. They come, to this last town on the long Cape, in good part for the very beauty that their numbers imperil. They come for fellowship, the beaches and the sun, the entertainment, the shops and restaurants. They inhabit old captains' houses turned into inns, or the condominiums ever rising along newly created streets and crowded cul-de-sacs. So, this is an elegy.

In the summers, black snakes swirled among the creamy blossoms of the honeysuckle and the pink-petaled roses. When I walked through the grass, their black faces appeared, like exotic flowers. There were almost always two of them, sometimes three. One had eyes the color of garnets. It gave no greeting, only a long, motionless gaze. And they were brave, those snakes. Occasionally when I came upon a pair sleeping in the sun, on stones or a heap of old asphalt shingles, one of them would streak toward me and fling itself against my body, before it turned and followed the other away, whipping after it into the shadows under the roses.

Soon they will be off, hunting another place to live. Which may not be so easy, for the world today is nothing if it is not sprawl, and this not only within the residential areas but the seemingly endless facilities such settlements need. And we do need them. (So, this is an elegy.) Box turtles nested here, and painted turtles also. Out of the shallow ponds below the crest of the hill, snapping turtles crawled to lay their pale, leathery eggs. Raccoons aspire to them; many of the nests were ransacked as soon as the turtle had shuffled away. Foxes left their dainty tracks, and in summer the red-coated deer.

The toad was always here, with his gold-rimmed eyes.

And, in a certain shaded place nearby, the uncommon, cool and gleaming bunchberry.

For years there were signs posted, prohibitions against leaving trash. In more recent years another sign designated the area a motorcycle and motorbike course. The bikes appeared most often in the afternoons; they snarled over the field, they cut ruts along the trails, they raced with a furious, uncontainable form of boyenergy and noise. I hated it, yet did not resent it. There must be a place for boys and their trappings, though surely it should not have been here, on one of the few town-owned woodlands fresh and untrammeled except for its polluted center. Also it joined seamlessly with the National Seashore, and what young boy hunched over the handlebars of his bike could remember that invisible line? So sections of the park's shady paths also became rutted by tires and besotted by blown trash. But when space is limited for recreations of such different kinds, compatibility is given improbable tasks.

As for the trash, which gathered in spite of the signs, it did what trash does and ever will do; it lay there, and did not grow thin or fade or even, much of it, rot. Old stoves were predominant. And dozens of tires, lining the bike track, the standing water within them breeding uncountable numbers of mosquitoes.

And yet, at certain hours, in the absence of boys and their bikes, I could walk here and see birds I found nowhere else: the indigo bunting, for example, and the black-billed cuckoo. And their more findable associates: goldfinches, catbirds, the brown thrasher, the yellowthroat, palm warblers, the grosbeak. The ruby-throated hummingbird nested here, but even now I will not tell you in precisely what tree. It was a secret to be kept then, so why not keep it still, now that the birds and the tree itself have vanished? And there were daisies, and butter-and-eggs, and milkweed with its mauve pendants, and Black-eyed Susans. There were rugosas, white and red. In the summer light they shot upward heavy with buds and pleated, glossy leaves. Then sagged under their own sweet weight.

But this is an elegy. Now there are buildings to take care of this new and important work. A brick building, neat and Cape Cod enough that it could almost be a bank! And behind it a huge, circular, cement construction—I cannot call it a building—round and thick-walled: not built for beauty, and not yet finished. Piles of pipes are everywhere. The blackberries that climbed up and down the hill, the goldenrod, the honeysuckle are gone; the pink roses are gone; the fox tracks are gone.

The land itself has been capped against the poisons that have been seeping all these years into the ground, from the fires, from the unknown elements cast away: oils and paints and car batteries and a hundred offensive substances more. And, imagine! for what unaware years I picked the blackberries and the raspberries, and thought them sweet and fine—thought them good fortune. And found, on the rubbled hillsides, strange shapes of old jars, glass bent and reshaped by the flames. Nuggets of deep blue from medicine containers; once a glass airplane that originally held candy, with a chip missing from one wing.

But, this is an elegy. A part of the book of not-wanting-to-let-go. And, go it must; and go it has. The pink roses and the toad with gold-rimmed eyes. The young boys on bikes who in fact are men now. Even the tires are gone. The town government has made its not unreasonable decision. We cannot continue with failing cesspools; we cannot condone seepage into the water supply, or into the blue harbor that lies along the town's frontage. And, we are so many.

In May the moccasin flowers blossomed, even in this thin soil, extravagantly. They stood in gatherings of six or seven, like small choirs getting ready to sing. Very rarely, one flower would rise pure white.

I do not like what has happened. I do not hold the loss lightly. I wish to be reasonable; I know I must be amenable to what is necessary. But—such few choices! I apologize to the hummingbird. I hope the snakes have found a new home. I hope the new system works. I am glad that I have a good memory; I will not forget the dainty tracks of the fox, or the goldfinches, or the everlasting. I think I know what our manifest, tree-filled, creature-lively world is—our garden and our pasture and our recreation. Also it is our schoolhouse, courthouse, church, graveyard, and the soft breath of eternity.

I walk in the world to love it. Only one question, really, frightens me. I wonder why, in all the years I walked in the old burn dump—this waste place, this secret garden—I never met another soul there, who had come forth for a like reason.

PART THREE

ARTISTS OF THE BEAUTIFUL

Emerson: An Introduction

THE DISTINCTION AND particular value of anything, or any person, inevitably must alter according to the time and place from which we take our view. In any new discussion of Emerson, these two weights are upon us. By time, of course, I mean our entrance into the twenty-first century; it has been two hundred years since Emerson's birth in Boston. By place, I mean his delivery from the town of Concord, and all his corporeal existence anywhere. Now he is only within the wider, immeasurable world of our thoughts. He lives nowhere but on the page, and in the attentive mind that leans above that page.

This has some advantage for us, for he is now the Emerson of our choice: he is the man of his own time—his own history—or he is one of the mentors of ours. Each of these possibilities has its attractions, for the man alive was unbelievably sweet and, for all his devotion to reason, wondrously spontaneous. Yet as time's passage has broken him free of all mortal events, we begin to know him more clearly for the labors of his life: the life of his mind. Surely he was looking for something that would abide beyond the Tuesday or the Saturday, beyond even his first powerful or cautionary or lovely effect. "The office of the scholar," he wrote in "The American Scholar," "is to cheer, to raise, and to guide men by showing them facts amidst appearances." The lofty fun of it is that his "appearances" were all merely material and temporal—brick walls, garden walls, ripening pears—while his facts were all of a shifty vapor and an unauthored goodwill—the luminosity of the pears, the musics of birds and the wind, the affirmative staring-out light of the night stars. And his belief that a man's inclination, once awakened to it, would be to turn all the heavy sails of his life to a moral purpose.

The story of his life, as we can best perceive it from its appearances, is as follows. Ralph Waldo Emerson was born in 1803; his father, William Emerson, died in 1811. The family—his mother, two sisters, and five brothers—were poor, devout, and intellectually ambitious. Death's fast or slow lightning was a too-frequent presence. Both girls and one boy died in childhood; Emerson's brothers William, Edward, and Charles survived only into early manhood. The only remaining brother to live a life of full length was Robert, who was a man of childish mind. Even as the poet Walt Whitman for most of his life took responsibility for his child-minded brother, Eddie, so did Emerson keep watch over this truculent survivor.

Emerson graduated from Harvard College, then divinity school, and in 1829 began preaching at the Second Church (Unitarian) in Boston. In that year also he married the beautiful but frail Ellen Tucker. Her health never improved, and in 1832 she died. Emerson was then twenty-nine years old.

I think it is fair to say that from this point on, the greater energies of his life found their sustenance in the richness and the steadfastness of his inner life. Soon after Ellen Tucker's death he left the pulpit. He had come to believe that the taking of the sacrament was no more, nor was meant to be more, than an act of spiritual remembrance. This disclosure he made to his congregation, who perhaps were grateful for his forthrightness but in all honesty did not wish to keep such a preacher. Soon after, Emerson booked passage to Europe. He traveled slowly across the continent and, finally, to England. He was deeply touched by the magnificence of the past, so apparent in the cities, in their art and architecture. He also made it his business to explore the present. The list of those with whom he met and talked is amazing: Coleridge, Wordsworth, Walter Savage Lander, and John Stuart Mill among them. His meeting with Thomas Carlyle began a lifelong friendship, their letters going back and forth across the Atlantic until Emerson's death in 1882.

Emerson returned from Europe and established a manner of living that he would scarcely alter for the rest of his life. He married again, a young woman named Lydia Jackson. In his journals, which he had begun in college and never abandoned, he tore down wall after wall in his search for a style and for ideas that would reach forth and touch both poles: his certainty and his fluidity. He bought a house in the town of Concord, an easy distance from Boston yet a place with its own extraordinary style and whose citizens were farmers, tradesmen, teachers, and the liveliest of utopians. Here, as husband and father, as writer and lecturer, Emerson would live for years his seemingly quiet, seemingly peaceful life.

The best use of literature bends not toward the narrow and the absolute but to the extravagant and the possible. Answers are no part of it; rather, it is the opinions, the rhapsodic persuasions, the engrafted logics, the clues that are to the mind of the reader the possible keys to his own self-quarrels, his own predicament. This is the crux of Emerson, who does not advance straight ahead but wanders to all sides of an issue; who delivers suggestions with a kindly gesture—who opens doors and tells us to look at things for ourselves. The one thing he is adamant about is that we *should* look—we *must* look—for that is the liquor of life, that brooding upon issues, that attention to thought even as we weed the garden or milk the cow.

This policy, if such it might be called, he established at the start. The first book he published was called *Nature*; in it he refers, with equal serenity, to "Nature" and to "nature." We understand clearly that by the first he means "this web of God"—everything that is not the mind uttering such words—yet he sets our lives down among the small-lettered noun as well, as though to burden us equally with the sublime and the common. It is as if the combination—the necessary honoring of both—were the issue of utmost importance. *Nature* is a text that is entirely about divinity and first purposes, a book of manners, almost, but for the inner man. It does not demean by diction or implication the life that we are most apt to call "real," but it presupposes the heart's spiritual awakening as the true work of our lives. That this might take place in as many ways as there are persons alive did not at all disturb Emerson, and that its occurrence was the beginning of paradise here among the temporal fields was one of his few unassailable certainties.

In 1836, at the issue of this initial volume, and in the first years following, he was a man scarcely known to the world. Descended from seven generations of preachers, in conventional terms a failed churchman himself, he held no more important post than his membership in the Concord volunteer Fire Association. If he tried to be at home among the stars, so, too, he strove to be comfortable in his own living room. Mentor to Thoreau and neighbor to Hawthorne, the idiosyncratic Bronson Alcott, the passionate Margaret Fuller, the talkative Ellery Channing, and the excitable Jones Very, he adorned his society with friendliness and participation. His house was often full of friends, and talk. Julian Hawthorne, then a young boy, remembers him sitting in the parlor, "legs crossed and—such was their flexibility—with one foot hitched behind the other ankle. Leaning forward, elbow on one knee, he faced his guests and held converse." There was an evening when his daughter Ellen called him away to talk to the butcher about mutton. It is reported that he rose mildly to do as he was bid. And there is another story—as he reported it himself in his journal, on a June day: "Now for near five years I have been indulged by the gracious Heaven in my long holiday in this goodly house of mine, entertaining and entertained by so many worthy and gifted friends, and all this time poor Nancy Barron, the mad-woman, has been screaming herself hoarse at the Poorhouse across the brook and I still hear her whenever I open my window."

Emerson was the leading member of the group we know as the New England transcendentalists. It is hardly a proper philosophy; certainly it is not a school of thought in which all members were in agreement. Impossible such a finding would have been with the various sensibilities of Concord! For each member, therefore, it must be reported somewhat differently. For Emerson, it devolved from Coleridge and German philosophy, from Swedenborg, no doubt from half a hundred other voices, as from his religious beliefs and his own appreciation of the world's more-than-utilitarian beauty. For Emerson, the value and distinction of transcendentalism was very much akin to this swerving and rolling away from acute definition. All the world is taken in through the eye, to reach the soul, where it becomes *more,* representative of a realm deeper than appearances: a realm ideal and sublime, the deep stillness *that is,* whose whole proclamation is the silence and the lack of material instance in which, patiently and radiantly, the universe exists. Emerson would not turn from the world, which was domestic, and social, and collective, and required action. Neither would he swerve from that unperturbable inner radiance, mystical, forming no rational word but drenched with passionate and untranslatable song. A man should want to be domestic, steady, moral, politic, reasonable. He should want also to be subsumed, whirled, to know himself as dust in the fingers of the wind. This was his supple, unbreakable faith.

His certainty that a man must live also in this world, enjoined with the similar faith of the other transcendentalists, was no small force in the New England of the 1830s and 1840s, especially in speech and action on behalf of abolition. Slow as he often was to express outrage, Emerson burst forth in his journal thus: "This filthy enactment [of the Fugitive Slave Law] was made in the 19th century, by people who could read and write. I will not obey it, by God." And he did not.

Writing that loses its elegance loses its significance. Moreover, it is no simple matter to be both inspirational and moderate. Emerson's trick—I use the word in no belittling sense—was to fill his essays with "things" at the same time that his subject was conceptual, invisible, no more than a glimmer, but a glimmer of immeasurable sharpness inside the eye. So he attached the common word to the startling idea. "Hitch your wagon to a star," he advised. "The drop is a small ocean." "A foolish consistency is the hobgoblin of little minds." "We live amid surfaces, and the true art of life is to skate well on them." "Sleep lingers all our lifetime about the eyes, as night hovers all day in the boughs of the fir tree." "The soul makes the body." "Prayer is the contemplation of the facts of life from the highest point of view," he says, and suddenly that elite mystical practice seems clearer than ever before, and possible to each of us.

    Of course his writing is made up of the nineteenth-century sentence, so nimble with commas. The sparks of his expression move forward softly and reasonably, in their shapely phrases—then they leap. He rests upon the gnomic as a poet will rest upon meter, and comes not to a conclusion but to a pause in which the reader's own impetus, given such a bright shove, takes over. And yet it is not ornamental eloquence, but natural, fecund, ripe, full of seed, and possibility. Even, or especially (it is his specialty, after all), when talking about the utterly unprovable, he sends out good news, as good reports come all day from the mockingbird, or the soft tongues of the Merrimack. The writing is a pleasure to the ear, and thus a tonic to the heart, at the same time that it strikes the mind.

Thus he wrote and lectured, often in Boston and New York but also as far west as Missouri and beyond. He did not especially like travel, or being away from home, but needed the money and trusted the lecturing process as a way for him to develop and polish his essays for eventual publication.

In 1847, Emerson, by then an established writer widely honored on both sides of the Atlantic, returned to England. The audiences for his lectures were large and curious. Crabb Robinson, in his diary of those years, relates first his own response and then the reaction of the writer Harriet Martineau:

> Tuesday, I heard Emerson's first lecture, "On the Laws of Thought;" one of those rhapsodical exercises of mind, like Coleridge's in his "Table Talk," and Carlyle's in his Lectures, which leave a dreamy sense of pleasure, not easy to analyze, or render an account of.... I can do no better than tell you what Harriet Martineau says about him, which, I think, admirably describes the character of his mind. "He is a man so *sui generis,* that I do not wonder at his not being apprehended till he is seen. His influence is of a curious sort. There is a vague nobleness and thorough sweetness about him, which move people to their very depths, without their being able to explain why. The logicians have an incessant triumph over him, but their triumph is of no avail. He conquers minds, as well as hearts, wherever he goes; and without convincing anybody's reason of any one thing, exalts their reason, and makes their minds worth more than they ever were before." 9TH JUNE, 1848.

That we are spirits that have descended into our bodies, of this Emerson was sure. That each man was utterly important and limitless, an "infinitude," of this he was also sure. And it was a faith that leads, as he shows us again and again, not to stasis but to activity, to the creation of the moral person from the indecisive person. Attachment to the Ideal, without participation in the world of men and women, was the business of foxes and flowers, not of men, not of women. This was, for Emerson himself, difficult. Outwardly he was calm, reasonable, patient. All his wildness was in his head—such a good place for it! Yet his certainty that thought, though it might grow most robust in the mind's repose, was sent and meant for participation in the world, never altered, never ebbed. There are, for myself, a hundred reasons why I would find my life—not only my literary, thoughtful life but my emotional, responsive life—impoverished by Emerson's absence, but none is greater than this unclosing of thought into the world's brilliant, perilous present. I think of him whenever I set to work on something worthy. And there he is also, avuncular and sweet, but firm and corrective, when I am below the mark. What we bring forth, he has taught me as deeply as any writer could, is predictable.

But let him have the last word. In his journal he wrote:

> I have confidence in the laws of morals as of botany. I have planted maize in my field every June for seventeen years and I never knew it come up strychnine. My parsley, beet, turnip, carrot, buck-thorn, chestnut, acorn, are as sure. I believe that justice produces justice, and injustice injustice.

Hawthorne's *Mosses from an Old Manse*

WHEN NATHANIEL HAWTHORNE began gathering his stories and sketches for *Mosses from an Old Manse,* he was living in Concord, Massachusetts, and in just such a house as he describes at the outset of the book. It was a sturdy house, built by Ralph Waldo Emerson's grandfather, the Reverend William Emerson. Some years earlier it had been lived in by Emerson himself, and here—very likely in the same room that Hawthorne describes[1]—Emerson completed his first book, *Nature*. One would have to look a long time—possibly forever—to find a house, or a chamber, that could claim an equal quantity of splendor

Hawthorne lived in Rev. Emerson's house from the summer of 1842 into the fall of 1845. In "The Old Manse" he tells us of the pleasure it brought him, and this is no small matter for a man who has left such an impression of his solemnity, who as a neighbor was remembered mostly for his silence, and who as a writer is known best for his aptitude in describing the darker portions of the soul. But clearly, in the writing chamber he was to use, made fresh and comfortable by his wife, Sophia, he was charmed:

> When I first saw the room, its walls were blackened with the smoke of unnumbered years, and made still blacker by the grim prints of Puritan ministers that hung around.

> These worthies looked strangely like bad angels, or, at least, like men who had wrestled so continually and so sternly with the devil, that somewhat of his sooty fierceness had been imparted to their own visages. They had all vanished now. A cheerful coat of paint, and golden-tinted paper-hangings, lighted up the small apartment; while the shadow of a willow tree, that swept against the overhanging eaves, attempered the cheery western sunshine.
> —"The Old Manse"

Hawthorne tells us that "The Old Manse" came slowly, and only with great difficulty. The rest of the tales and sketches were arranged; publication waited for these delicate and sweet-tempered paragraphs, this welcome into the man's residence, and with that welcome a kind of opening of the heart. The sketch is long; it is not profound, nor mystical, nor does it hold any single theme; yet it is the revelatory piece in the book. In it we meet a Hawthorne rarely otherwise disclosed. Think of *The Scarlet Letter* and *The House of the Seven Gables:* the shadows, the sins, the moral retributions, the gravity, the import. The somber intentions of those books would never allow us to imagine Hawthorne's capacity for gladness and for idling, the cordiality and the enthusiasm he felt toward the surrounding natural world, toward friendship, even toward the ghosts of the old manse, one of whom he describes with both probity and humor:

> Houses of any antiquity, in New England, are so invariably possessed with spirits, that the matter seems hardly worth alluding to. Our ghost used to heave deep sighs in a particular corner of the parlor, and sometimes rustled paper, as if he were turning over a sermon, in the long upper entry;—where, nevertheless, he was invisible, in spite of the bright moonshine that fell through the eastern window. Not improbably, he wished me to edit and publish a selection

> from a chest full of manuscript discourses, that stood in the garret.
>
> —"The Old Manse"

—

Hawthorne was born on July 4, 1804, in the old port town of Salem, Massachusetts. He and two sisters were the children of Elizabeth Clarke Manning and Nathaniel Hathorne,[2] a ship captain. The children were still young when Captain Hathorne perished, in a distant part of the world, of an unnamed fever; the family was left poor, and none of them, certainly not Nathaniel's mother, owned the gift of disarming such loss. Religious devotion and spiritual gloom need not necessarily cling together, but in the Hathorne household, from all we can discover, they were inseparable.

Nathaniel grew up physically active and strikingly handsome; he was also, for good reason, shy, and probably lonely. In 1825 he graduated from Bowdoin College in Maine, then returned to Salem. Residents of the town frequently saw him, in the late afternoons, roaming along the streets and the shore: a solitary wanderer. One may with confidence record that he was steadfast; for a decade he continued to live in his mother's house, where he worked at his writing, finishing stories he later burned and one novel that made not the slightest noise in the literary world. Then he met the Peabody sisters of Salem, and with one of them, Sophia, he fell in love. Five years later, in 1842, they married. They were, Hawthorne wrote to a friend, close to "ridiculous" in their happiness.

—

Such happiness, however, neither writes nor sells stories. After the publication of the novels for which he is most widely known, his financial situation would improve—somewhat. Still, as we know, he held the position of surveyor at the Salem Custom House and the finer appointment of American Consul in England even later, for no other reason, at either opportunity, than his need for financial security. One can imagine, then, the difficulty of supporting his family, which soon contained three children, in the early years. He was publishing stories, but the "fame" of being an author was not golden enough, nor silver either. Payment was meager, and in Hawthorne's case, as we learn from his correspondence, often it was no more than visionary.

For this reason, which is neither glorious nor inglorious but very real, his collecting of stories for *Mosses* was not the gathering of a man secure enough, in this world, to pick and choose, or to wait. The invitation to publish the book had come in 1845, and he intended to fulfill it. Hawthorne had written much and well in the writing chamber in the old manse, and the major part of *Mosses* represents work produced during that time. Except for the opening piece, he wrote nothing new. He used what existed—not all of it, certainly, but his intent was to fill the pages. The result is a book with an extraordinary breadth of styles; here are dark, brooding tales, arch and humorous sketches, and stories of a curiously intense allegorical slant; here also are writings that have their genesis in Hawthorne's own experiences, or ideas, or reminiscences. Among the most striking of his stories—I am thinking of "The Birthmark," "Young Goodman Brown," "Rappaccini's Daughter," and "The Artist of the Beautiful" in particular—these sketches are interspersed, composed in the flute-note of rapture or the little triangle clatter of praise: "Passages from a Relinquished Work," "Sketches from Memory," "Buds and Bird Voices," "The Old Apple Dealer," and also the robust meditation "Fire Worship." One may look at such a collection of writings either way—one may say: but no invisible magnet, or idea, holds these choice particles; how can it then be a book, which is surely more than a simple gathering of accomplishments? Or, just as easily—if one is not staked to the rules—one may say: what variety, what richness!

—

Hawthorne is one of the great imaginers of evil, and also of its henchmen: lassitude, doubt, despair, unmitigated ambition—all varieties of human weakness and vanity that wreck the work of conscience. It is his primary theme, the instructing of the malicious toward its various appearances. Hawthorne's heritage was pure Salem, and not just his mother's house—it was his own great-great-grandfather William Hathorne who ordered the whipping of Anne Coleman and four other Friends through the streets of Salem; and it was his great-grandfather John Hathorne who sat magistrate at the trial of the accused witches of Salem. The shadow of this history could not fail to reach into the nineteenth century to darken Nathaniel Hawthorne. The Puritan strain was his—not to live by, as his forbears did, but to brood upon, to examine, to explore.

From it came the novels *The Scarlet Letter* and *The House of the Seven Gables*. Also from the dreadful pall of this history came the turbulent "Young Goodman Brown," very likely his most widely known story. It casts into that old shadow in an attempt to find, I think, the point—the exact point—at which the soul is captured, and how, and why. Young Goodman Brown simply sets off into the forest on an unnamed errand. We have no notion what sort of journey this is, yet we feel his own wretched uneasiness as the appearances of things, and people, previously reliable, begin to be proven—or believed—false. It is vitally unnerving. "Young Goodman Brown" is not really a story about the perturbation of the actual—the "witches" that sweep across the air, the walking stick that writhes like a serpent; it is about the human heart that, imagining awful things, is responsive to them, and so falls into a pollution and dismay of the mind. The "satanic" theatrics may even be conceived as the leitmotif, compared with the horror of Goodman Brown's spiritual failing. Nor does Hawthorne expend any measure of words of pity for Goodman Brown's fate. The story stands, simply, as an adjudication for spiritual strength.

In "The Birthmark," the malevolent force develops from something admirable gone awry—the desire for knowledge and its attendant power, unsoftened by human warmth; the same force appears equally if not more sinister in "Rappaccini's Daughter." In "Roger Malvin's Burial," a decent man is brought to a life of distress by a moment of deceit, in which he does not tell the truth but fabricates an action he wished to but did not accomplish; the retribution is without mercy. Such stories are Hawthorne's finest, and they are Puritan in this sense: they are harsh, unrelenting, and fearful in their certainty. But they are also something else, for the origin of Hawthorne's certainty is not that of the Puritan within his religious confines, but that of the humanist who sees the moral actions of the conscience as the creator of good or evil. In this grand alteration of his inheritance, Hawthorne is timelessly alive, compassionate, elastic, and modern.

Still, a reader may desire relief from such seriousness, and be glad therefore that in another tone altogether Hawthorne plays with fantasy, creating the airy landscapes of a half-dozen stories in which the sky is literally the limit: one may walk upon the pale clouds into fantastic marble halls, or vast, improbable castles, or ride in a celestial train to the very edge of heaven. These stories are serious but not somber. They are parables perhaps, but they flow forward in so likable a manner they are able to review the weaknesses and absurdities of humankind without hurt, or the weight we feel with pedantic judgment. Perhaps, of this type of story, the beautiful "Monsieur du

Miroir" is the most successful, in which, with sparkling good humor, Hawthorne describes that other man who follows him everywhere there is a water or a mirror surface.

> One of this singular person's most remarkable peculiarities is his fondness for water, wherein he excels any temperanceman whatever.... When no cleaner bathing-place happened to be at hand, I have seen the foolish fellow in a horse-pond. Sometimes he refreshes himself in the trough of a townpump, without caring what the people think about him. Often, while carefully picking my way along the street, after a heavy shower, I have been scandalized to see M. du Miroir, in full dress, paddling from one mud-puddle to another, and plunging into the filthy depths of each. Seldom have I peeped into a well, without discerning this ridiculous gentleman at the bottom, whence he gazes up, as through a long telescopic tube, and probably makes discoveries among the stars by daylight. Wandering along lonesome paths, or in pathless forests, when I have come to virgin-fountains, of which it would have been pleasant to deem myself the first discoverer, I have started to find M. du Miroir there before me. The solitude seemed lonelier for his presence.
>
> —Monsieur du Miroir

Of that light and lovely tone, in order to understand Hawthorne, we must speak more. For it is greatly from his unfailing capacity to write the sweetest prose—and to create with it a virtual atmosphere—that his stories take breath and live. Often enough the forward action is slight, or obvious, and the characters but scantily drawn. But the surround, the detail, is deep and luxurious. Henry James wrote of Hawthorne, "He thought nothing too trivial to be suggestive."[3] Such a style is not unique to Hawthorne, nor to the nineteenth century; some of Poe's work is equally shaded and embellished by scenery and setting, and it carries as much of the weight of the story as the action. "The Tell-Tale Heart" is one, "The Black Cat" another; "The Pit and the Pendulum" leaps to the list. Hemingway's "Big Two-Hearted River," in which a man simply goes fishing, is another story in which every leaf and ripple of the atmosphere adds to its import, its weight and pressure—its reality. Our own era more commonly offers a brisker prose, with a more complex plot, or plots, threading along, and much of the surround left to the imagination. The difference is neither plus nor minus, of course, but simply one of the alternations which readers must allow as they begin to climb the delectable mountains of old books.

—

Hawthorne began his consulship in England in 1853; when it was over, he spent two years traveling on the continent and lived for a while in Italy. He and Sophia and the children returned to New England in 1860, and immediately took up residence in another Concord house, known as the Wayside Inn. He was by then the author of four novels and a number of collections of stories. His fame was established, his readers were many, and his literary peers acknowledged him among the foremost writers of his time. He had laid out ideas for and had begun work on two new novels.

But fate had other ideas. Sturdy and vigorous and seemingly full of shining health he had always been; now he began to show signs of decline. No one has given a name to what was wrong, but all saw it; his hair turned white, his energy flagged, his spirit struggled. In his sixtieth year he died while on a trip in New Hampshire where he had gone hoping to recruit his old health once again. He was brought to Sleepy Hollow, Concord's green and lush burial ground. There, already, were more than a few men he had known, Thoreau among them. Julian, Hawthorne's son, remembered riding with his mother through the Sleepy Hollow gates after the burial ceremony. "There, on each side of the way, stood men with gray heads and lowered eyes."[4] The men, standing there to pay homage, were Longfellow, Holmes, Emerson, Franklin Pierce,[5] Whittier, and Lowell.

Probably the years spent in Concord were Hawthorne's happiest. He worked well there, and for all his taciturnity he liked being part of Concord's select and neighborly society. One friend was Ellery Channing; on any day Channing might arrive at the old manse, and the two friends would go off together:

> Strange and happy times were those, when we cast aside all irksome forms and straight-laced habitudes, and delivered ourselves up to the free air, to live like the Indians or any less conventional race, during one bright semi-circle of the sun. Rowing our boat against the current, between wide meadows, we turned aside into the Assabeth. A more lovely stream than this, for a mile above its junction with the Concord, has never flowed on earth—nowhere, indeed, except to lave the interior regions of a poet's imagination.
> —"The Old Manse"

No writer is capable of a more tender expressiveness than Hawthorne. In his craft he has the thoughtful charm that is the lighter element of intellect. He has also that gravity which is the pace of moral purpose. In his steadfastness he is another Owen Warland, who, in "The Artist of the Beautiful," feels alive only when striving, not to demystify beauty, but to commit himself to its spiritual requirements.

In no other book of his, I think, does Hawthorne pass on to us such a sense of the thoughtful, cheerful, easy-hearted atmosphere of his life. Here only, along with his probing tales of evil, we are given stories full of wit and sunshine, which are, though Hawthorne lacked the poet's cadence, created throughout with a poet's skill.

The House of the Seven Gables

All three of the essays in this part of the book were written initially as introductions for the Modern Library Classics series. I beg the reader's indulgence for material, in this third essay, that repeats information concerning Hawthorne's history and life. It goes by fast, and was necessary, of course, to this separate introduction.

WITH EVERY PASSING year the great old novels grow more quaint, but no less spectacular. The characters in Nathaniel Hawthorne's *The House of the Seven Gables* have about them certain casual differences from us—their clothes, the slight tarnish of their gentility, a little stiffness in their conversation. We read, at first, about *them*; it is *their* story. But there are few stories in the world, after all. There is the story of Wickedness, the story of Good, the story of Love, and the story of Time. It is the telling that is the charm, for it is the expression that gives to our imaginations the experience of the tale. And that, surely, is the singular gift of every good book: the scenes and moments—the "fancy pictures," as Hawthorne calls them—that with their prolonged and indelible coloration convey again the joy and anguish of distant landscapes. Though the present century is sparkling new, we must enter the old books not with a rude curiosity but with a realization that beneath surface differences the characters are not strange, they are not different; they are *exactly* ourselves. And the stories that offer a real entertainment do not stop there. We realize them also as portions of a communal narrative, as one story after another displays—for literature is about displaying, not hiding—old hopes and clarities, old passions and transgressions, old charities and judgments.

And there is of course the actual writing itself. Every age develops its peculiarities and distinctions of style. Books of our own time favor a kind of fly-by posture; they are frequently built of briskness and implication rather than detail. *The House of the Seven Gables* was published in 1851, at the center of the nineteenth century. Most books of that period take their good old time—*The House of the Seven Gables* certainly does. One could write out the events that unfold in its pages with fewer words than Hawthorne uses in some of the most static—yet marvelous, poetic, and deeply resonant—scenes in the book. They reveal Hawthorne as one of the sweetest prose stylists of his time. They are almost paintings, and they are written for the long and searching look. Like the great, black house itself, they offer up their meanings slowly, as the hours turn and the light changes and the mind begins to read in a kind of largo of sympathy.

The old house, in the damp and flowing east wind, its roof roughened by mosses and even flowers, stands at the center of the tale. Its task now is merely to endure, to shelter present poverty and melancholy as, in the past, it sheltered power and pride. Like another unforgettable and depressing structure, in Edgar Allan Poe's "The Fall of the House of Usher," it is an emblem of the life within. "The aspect of the venerable mansion has always affected me like a human countenance," says the narrator at the start of Hawthorne's tale. This is not greatly different from the beginning of Poe's story, in which the narrator looks upon the scene, "upon the mere house, and the simple landscape features of the domain—upon the bleak walls—upon the vacant eye-like windows—upon a few rank sedges ... with an utter depression of soul." The depths to which one falls from that "utter depression" is the subject of Poe's stories over and over again. His characters plunge into the caverns of the mind, to its display of amazing and often horrifying complexities and irregularities. All Hawthorne's effort, from a similar melancholy, is in another direction. The soul itself is not Hawthorne's subject, but the soul and its brother souls, and its sister souls: "Persons who have wandered, or been expelled, out of the common track of things, even were it for a better system, desire nothing so much as to be led back. They shiver in their loneliness, be it on a mountain-top or in a dungeon."

While the House of Usher tumbles toward oblivion, the House of the Seven Gables stands, for its occupants make small but important gestures of resistance. They do not wish to be irregular; they desire re-entrance into the world. For them the ordinary is glossed in the finest light, and human decency is crucial. Although they have had no power against the wickedness that has pressed upon them, they know it for what it is. It is the fineness of this certainty—this decisive sense of what should be and what should not be—that makes them so appealing, and their tale so timelessly relevant. Moral transgression is Hawthorne's central subject. Inevitably, the tensions between goodness and wickedness, and between society and the individual, are never far from that center. In *The House of the Seven Gables,* Hawthorne's subject more particularly is the corruption of power and the almost endlessly inherited tendency to its continuance. It is, also, about the possibility or impossibility of reparation. It is, therefore, about the future being held hostage by the past. But most of all, it is about lives caught in the common fire of history.

In an extraordinary and savage pocket of the seventeenth century, 1690 exactly, the Puritan community of New England—in Salem,

Massachusetts, precisely—plunged into a seemingly unquenchable hysteria that ended in "the work of blood." The Puritan community "discovered" among its population certain persons, men and women both, whom they declared, by trial, to be witches, and whom they condemned to die. Before the horror was over nineteen men and women were hanged. A twentieth man died while being tortured, a scene readers of Arthur Miller's play *The Crucible,* based on these events, will not easily forget.

The men and women were hanged and buried in the stony surround of Gallows Hill. All protested their innocence and, in one case at least, expressed their wrath. It is recalled that Sarah Good, before she died, cursed one of the judges aloud: "God will give you blood to drink," she cried. Another of the judges was a man named John Hathorne.

There is in Hawthorne's story a powerful and merciless judge who is descended from a man who was one of the witchcraft-trial judges. Clearly and importantly, we are meant to feel the long shadow. Characters in books are not ever actual people living or dead, not quite, and events do not become a narrative, not exactly. It is, as Hawthorne says, "a mixing." In this case it must have been a mixing, for him, of singular poignancy and weight, for the John Hathorne who took part in the Salem trials was the great-great-grandfather of Nathaniel Hawthorne the writer.

In the society of Concord, Massachusetts, a hundred and fifty years after these events, Thoreau was independent and cocksure; Emerson was brilliant and enigmatic. Hawthorne was the broody man. He seemed able to enter no more than the edges of society, even in the cordiality of Concord. His son Julian would write years later of wandering through the fields and woods with Thoreau. But of his father he recalled, "He didn't drink, or care for tobacco; on the whole he preferred looking on to joining in, and could exercise a gift of silence." Emerson and Hawthorne, though they were courteous, and though Emerson, with others, gave assistance when Hawthorne and his bride, Sophia Peabody, moved into the old manse in Concord, were able to form no lasting or deep relationship. The journals of each man give evidence of this holding back. It had to do with their differences of thought and work as well as their unmatchable sensibilities, no doubt. But in any case Hawthorne was a man steeped in solitude, and except for friendships made during his college years and for his relationship with Sophia, he remained so.

His life story does little to release us from this sense of a man alone with his thoughts, and alone in the universe. He was born on July 4, 1804, in Salem, Massachusetts. His father, Nathaniel Hathorne, was a ship captain who died half the world away when the boy was young. His youth, except for his years at Bowdoin College, was spent with his mother and his two sisters in their Salem home, and if he or any of them was merry at times, we have no news of it. Until her own death, his mother, according to custom, dressed in black and took her meals by herself in her own room. True, Hawthorne had uncles and other relatives, and like any boy he took part in sports and school activities. But he returned always to this house, where, after graduating from Bowdoin, he spent day after day in his own room—a decade of days—reading and writing. In the evenings, he took long walks alone. "Castle Dismal" he called the house. "In the last ten years I have not lived, but only dreamed of living," he once wrote to a friend.

He began to publish stories and also a novel, *Fanshawe*, which went unnoticed in the world. Then, a stroke of the best, sweetest good fortune: his sisters introduced him to a neighboring family, the Peabodys—three young women—and one of them, Sophia, he married five years later. Sophia Peabody made no secret of her happiness to be married to "this very king and poet of the world."

One of Hawthorne's classmates at Bowdoin College was Franklin Pierce, later President Pierce. Perhaps it was a mixed blessing, this deepest of Hawthorne's friendships. While running for the office of president, Pierce asked Hawthorne to write his campaign biography, which Hawthorne did. Necessarily, he presented Pierce's views in a favorable light, including a statement on slavery (an institution Pierce was willing to leave intact). Such writing could not have enhanced relationships with his abolitionist neighbors in Concord.

The question of benefit or disruption stemming from the friendship between Pierce and Hawthorne is unanswerable, but the question is there. When Pierce became president, he offered Hawthorne the position of American consul in Liverpool, England, a busy and important post. Hawthorne by this time had published his two best-known works, *The Scarlet Letter* (1850) and *The House of the Seven Gables* (1851), as well as *The Wonder Book* (1851), *The Blithedale Romance* (1852), *The Snow Image, and Other Twice-Told Tales*, (1852), and *Tanglewood Tales* (1853). His reputation as a writer was established and growing; it was a risky moment for interruption. It was also the first time Hawthorne felt he could give his family, which now included three young children, security and comfort. He accepted the consular position, and held it for five years, from 1853 to 1858. During this period, he accomplished almost nothing in the way of writing.

At the election of a new president, Hawthorne was replaced. The family spent another two years in Europe, living primarily in Italy, before they returned to America and to Concord. But the vitality of the writer Hawthorne was, it would appear, not renewable. He completed a novel, *The Marble Faun* (1860). In the next years he began but failed to finish two final works, *Septimus Felton* and *The Dolliver Romance*.

For Hawthorne now, it was twilight. His health declined. Always chary of doctors, he would seek no professional advice.

Sophia finally asked Oliver Wendell Holmes, as a friend and a medical man, to judge what he could of Hawthorne's condition. Holmes said nothing definite to Sophia; privately he reported: "The shark's tooth is on him." In the spring Hawthorne set out with Pierce, now the ex-president, for a journey through New England, a trip designed by Pierce to improve Hawthorne's condition if possible. But Hawthorne did not survive the journey; he died in his sleep in a hotel in Plymouth, New Hampshire, where the two old friends were staying. It was May 19, 1864. Hawthorne was fifty-nine years old.

In *The House of the Seven Gables* Hawthorne uses, as a distant but essential stage, a fictive retelling of the Puritan madness, in which a citizen of the unnamed town, Matthew Maule, is hanged as a witch. His accuser, a Colonel Pyncheon, who has for some time coveted Maule's two or three acres, comes into possession of them after Maule's death. Upon this rough ground the iron-hearted Pyncheon builds his house, and Hawthorne his dark story.

Besides the horror of the witchcraft hysteria itself, no reader will miss the implication of moral corruption that comes into existence with the original hammering together of the seven gables. Hawthorne's point is simple but runs as deep as men's hearts: the effect of such corruption may be—in fact, will be—inherited, along with all the visible amassments of the powerful and the rich, and it is a dreadful inheritance. After the completion of Colonel Pyncheon's house upon Matthew Maule's land, a spring that formerly offered the sweetest water turns sour—altered, it is suggested, not by nature but by the wickedness that has taken place. It has been, ever since Maule's death, "productive of intestinal mischief to those who quench their thirst there."

It is a theatrical moment. Indeed, among the events of the novel there are many moments of theatricality. The characters too are sometimes theatrical enough that it is tempting to read them with more than a touch of allegory, in this Romance in which human vice and virtue hold their long-standing contest. It is no great surprise that *Pilgrim's Progress* was one of Hawthorne's favorite books.

Hepzibah Pyncheon is such a paragon of fortitude and loyalty that she could represent in our minds these attributes alone, save for the exquisite and telling details drawn by Hawthorne to help us see and feel this steadfast life: Miss Hepzibah Pyncheon steps "into the dusky, time-darkened passage; a tall figure, clad in black silk, with a long and shrunken waist, feeling her way toward the stairs like a near-sighted person, as in truth she is." Poor, sensitive, white-haired Clifford Pyncheon, whose life has been ransacked and who can hardly speak above a whisper, astonishes us suddenly by his brief excitations. First he attempts to leap from a window in order to join the gathering of people below, a symbolic as well as a perilous act; later, setting the whole house ajar, he cries aloud, "I want my happiness! ... I want my happiness!"—every man's natural, though it be an impossible, desire.

The young Phoebe is all quickness and delight; she is anything but odd, peculiar, extraordinary. She alone is not past-possessed. "Phoebe, and the fire that boiled the teakettle, were equally bright, cheerful, and efficient, in their respective offices," writes Hawthorne. She is the unfettered future or, at least, its possibility. Holgrave is also of the future. He is patient and skillful, he is modern and savvy. Nowhere in *The House of the Seven Gables* is nature itself, in its uncombed and original state, of consequence to the ongoing drama; this is a book totally about the nature of man. Holgrave labors to restore the neglected gardens in back of the great house. He also takes photographs and, it is made clear that his skill, not merely the sunlight, is in this labor the essential and defining agent.

Judge Pyncheon, descendant of the old colonel, is, as we might expect, well dressed, well fed, well housed, well fawned upon; he struts when he walks, he gleams when he perspires, when he travels about the town holding in his breast a secret that has for years broadcast wreckage over other lives. Again and again it is Hawthorne's word for him: he is an "iron-hearted" man.

Eventually Judge Pyncheon will return to the old black house. Culmination is part of theater, and it is necessary to Hawthorne's ultimate intimation: moral error may be chastened, and upon the ashes of its awful cost, the future may be wrestled from the past. Such freedom, to go forward without moral culpability or moral injury, is what *The House of the Seven Gables* seeks and, insofar as it is humanly possible, finds, with time, courage, and the assistance of the great elf Death. When the judge returns to the house we sense that something terrible will be laid to rest, at last.

The House of the Seven Gables is a moral tale, and moral tales as we know have a tendency to be tedious. Piety is not much of a spice. But Hawthorne created, in Hepzibah and Clifford especially, characters so worn and odd, yet so firm, that we dare not mock their oddness lest in doing so we insult their decency. At the same time, along with the vanity and prosperity of Judge Pyncheon we must consider the misfortune of his inheritance, and the continuance of that misfortune. In the higher order of things—and all great books are about such elevation—it is the powerful, wealthy judge who is the shivering outcast, from family, from friendship, from love, and from true labor, all the things that make life round and shining. Imagine thinking money and dinner, malice and self-importance, all day long! "Unless you have lived a moral life you have lived no life at all," said Hawthorne's old friend Emerson. Hawthorne certainly would have agreed. And thus we see the judge not only as wicked but also as pathetic, absent, unalive: And we come to see Hepzibah and Clifford, those sufferers, for what they are. They have crossed the desert; they have reached the pole; they have flown to the moon! They are moral. They are heroic.

There is at the end of the book no going back, no retrieval but only, finally, settlement and release. What is attained is the one possible gift—the chance to begin anew, with youth and love, with hope and honor. One wishes for more. But evil has, like everything else, a past tense that cannot be erased. Wickedness, we see—but the Judge does not—is not simply an action against, it is a ravishment of, other lives. At its heart, the story of *The House of the Seven Gables* is about the sweetness of moral order, and the sourness—the terrible and prolonged bitterness—of its lack.

PART FOUR

DUST

Prose Poem: Are You Okay?

A small spider had crawled into the keyhole of the door. I fetched it out, carefully, and put it in my window with a bit of leaf, where she—if it was she—could catch the wind's not-so-soft talk, and plan the rest of her life.

For a long time she was motionless. Or so it seemed, for I don't know what adventures she might have risked in the night. Nor do I know whether, in the day hours, she was unable to move, or waiting for something to happen, or, simply, asleep.

She finally grew a small bottle-body, and ran a few strands up and down the screen. And then, one morning, she was gone.

It's a hot and dusty world. Glimmering, and dangerous. Once a little jumping spider, on a porch railing, came to my hand, and stood up on its back legs and stared, with exquisite green eyes, into my face. You can say that it wasn't so; it was so. This was on a warm summer day. A few sailboats were gliding around the harbor that stretches out and becomes the ocean, and who knows where the world ends. Good luck, little spider of the keyhole. Live as long as you can.

Poem: Softest of Mornings

Softest of mornings, hello.
And what will you do today, I wonder,
    to my heart?
And how much honey can the heart stand, I wonder,
    before it must break?

This is trivial, or nothing: a snail
    climbing a trellis of leaves
        and the blue trumpets of its flowers.

No doubt clocks are ticking loudly
    all over the world.
I don't hear them. The snail's pale horns
    extend and wave this way and that
as her finger-body shuffles forward, leaving behind
    the silvery path of her slime.

Oh, softest of mornings, how shall I break this?
How shall I move away from the snail, and the flowers?
How shall I go on, with my introspective and ambitious life?

Dust

1.

M. WOULD KEEP everything. There is not an envelope, with its singular name, address (best if written by-hand), postmark, and stamp that she would not keep, though the envelope be empty. To M. its emptiness does not reduce the envelope to irrelevance. Of course she would rather there be something inside—a letter! or, oh lovely chance, a photograph!—but even without these treasures and pleasures the envelope is a part of the mystery to be cherished. What was it the envelope held, to whom was it sent and why, and what did it matter? M. is both a sleuth and a shepherd. She would know all stories that are gone now, dispersed to the wind, to the ages, through layers of uncaring, lost in pigeonholes in the backs of abandoned desks, or the files of defunct institutions, or the sagging brown boxes in yard sales in summer, in distant towns, bought at last for a dollar or a song, and put into someone's car and driven off, or—unsold at the end of the long warm day—carried up the stairs and put back, for another season, under the eaves of the old barn. From none of this can M. back away, or remain indifferent. And, not letters only but things—old clothes, hats, mirrors with a streak of tarnish, books so old and dry they have summoned toward themselves every possible blot of moisture, so that they are swollen and unshuttable now forever, though they have become dry as bone again. Things! Chiffon, and lace, and bruised velvet. Shoes, with tiny buttons along the sides. And photographs, the unnameable faces gazing out, everything to say and no way, no way ever again, to be heard.

2.

It is five o'clock or maybe earlier on a winter morning when I come down the stairs. The sky is black, but not for long. I make coffee and walk from window to window, lifting the shades, watching the pink, tangerine, apricot, lavender light dart and sail along the eastern horizon, then climb like a mist and tremble there, on the inner curve of the darkness. The intimacy of the universe! The colors float down into the water, everything turns blue. Black ducks are dabbling near the rocks. Even now, in winter, many of them remain together in affectionate pairs. Flocks of brant move by, those elegant, small geese. The light grows stronger, whiter, the pinks and rouges fade as the sun hesitates, then leaps from the water. Gulls are already in the air.

In spring these sunrises will continue, beyond the blue iris and the pink mallow of the garden. Laughing gulls will fly by the house, with the black faces of spring. Black-bellied plovers feed along the shallows. In April, humpbacked whales sometimes swim into the harbor, tossing as they move their huge bodies forward. Dolphins come too, leaping through the waves.

Surf scoters come near the house, and the common eider and the gentle-eyed old squaw. A red-throated loon appears one morning just in front of the house; like a small torpedo it dashes down through the clear water.

In the summer common terns and least terns gather in the afternoon to feed, dropping, and dropping, and dropping again into the waves. The wings of each one are like two white petals on the rise; they give a quick shake to shed water, a break in the rhythm of the bird ascending.

Of course there are storms too, when the whole house rocks and the waves upbeat on the underside of the deck-boards, and sometimes win, and the wind sizzles, and you had better be on the ocean's side then, or you would be afraid.

In late summer, one or two small dogfish often swam near us. And, once, a pair of swans.

Then the summer would pass, and the long fall, and winter would swell around us again, and we would breathe deep and slow as we did our work in this crooked old seaside house that, for a little while, was ours.

3.

For the first time in twenty-five years there is no small footstool next to the bed, on which to break one's toes. The little dogs, first Jasper and then Bear, are gone. How neatening is loss, since it only takes away! One less mouth to feed, to walk, to bathe, to hold. One less sentient creature to cherish, to worry over, to feel for, to receive comfort from. And where is he, little Bear, the latest to leave us? We watch the white clouds carefully; sooner or later we will see him, sailing away in careless and beautiful serenity. Of what rich and ornate stuff the powerful and uncontainable gods invented the world, out of the rampant dust! The silky brant, the scarf of chiffon, the letter, the empty envelope, the black ducks, the old shoes, the little white dog fall away, fall away, and all the music of our lives is in them. The gods act as they act for what purpose we do not know, but this we do understand: the world could not be made without the swirl and whirlwind of our deepest attention and our cherishing. And if I mean the god of the sky, I mean also the god of the river—not only the god of the gold-speckled cathedral but the lord of the green field, where people pause casually and snap each other's picture; where thrushes release their darkling songs; where little dogs bark and leap, their ears tossing, joyously, as they run toward us.

Sand Dabs, Seven[1]

There is no pencil in the world that doesn't have the ability to strike out as well as to instigate. It's best to write, to begin with, generously.

～

If tone is wrong, nothing is right.

～

Lassitude in the heart puts lassitude on the page.

～

The sun has a working schedule, and the snow, and the birds, and every green leaf. Perhaps you should have one too?

～

No matter how cunning the sentence, it is impossible to hide pique.

～

Some writing should be set aside and forgotten. Maybe it needed more salt and pepper. Or, maybe, less.

～

Too many words, even the right words, can kill the poem.

～

Sometimes you will feel, like nothing else, the sweet, electric drowse of creation.

～

But sometimes you must bear the failure of labor to its anticipated result.

—

Plain as a needle a poem may be, or opulent as the shell of the channeled whelk, or the face of the lily, it matters not; it is a ceremony of words, a story, a prayer, an invitation, a flow of words that reaches out and, hopefully, without being real in the way that the least incident is real, is able to stir in the reader a real response.

—

Above all, take a chance. Sing, like blood going down the vein.

Poem: The Morning Walk

There are a lot of words meaning *thanks*.
Some you can only whisper.
Others you can only sing.
The pewee whistles instead.
The snake turns in circles,
the beaver slaps his tail
on the surface of the pond.
The deer in the pinewoods stamps his hoof.
Goldfinches shine as they float through the air.
A person, sometimes, will hum a little Mahler.
Or put arms around old oak tree.
Or take out lovely pencil and notebook to find a few
touching, kissing words.

Sand Dabs, Eight

The sharp-edged, glittering tens, the hours with locks on them; the hard twenties; the easing thirties; the fretful forties; the fifties, occasional hours of hope and promise, holding on. Now, the sixties.

―

And I would like to be simple and devout, like the oak tree.

―

And to tell the truth, sometimes I would like to be able to bark like a dog, to whistle like the meadowlark, to play a little banjo, like the frog in the summer pond.

―

Said M. in her sleep, "I want more money." Or was it, "I want more honey"?

―

The ants rush toward sweetness. I take away the melon, but first I spill a little melon juice on the counter.

―

Writing is only writing. The accomplishments of courage and tenderness are not to be measured by paragraphs.

―

I said to the grasshopper bounding along the road—how excellent you are at what you do!

―

The snapping turtle wore the most horrifying face I have ever seen, yet she seemed to be enjoying the warmth of the sun, as thoroughly as the household cat.

~

Twice in my life, not once, I have heard the wild wood duck call her hatchlings down from the tree nest. God is lavish.

~

The fur behind the mouse's ear stuns the finger with its softness.

~

When in the distance the town clock tapped out its brief news—Ah, three o'clock, I thought involuntarily, and felt one or two grains of my spirit die.

~

Today I saw the veery, up in the shadows, twirling his harp-whistle.

~

What would it be like to live one whole day as a Ruskin sentence, wandering like a creek with little comma bridges?

Comfort

I WOKE IN the night and heard the rain. No more sleep then, at least for a while, so wholeheartedly did I lie and listen. For doesn't the rain descend to us importantly? What have we, in the whole theater of our inventiveness—all five continents of it—so wonderful as this machinery of the wild world: water, falling out of the sky! The wheat and the lilies grow, or don't grow, depending on it. In autumn the trees fairly blind us with their color if the year's rain has been generous. The ponds freshen, or dry to a mere succulence—marshlands or even deserts—if rain has not come richly enough, or if it has come not at all.

I listened deeply; I also listened convivially. For the rain has a voice particular to the site it visits, and the way it touches the surface of the harbor here, and the undulations of sand, and the bayberries, is different from the lusher sounds of lowland rain or even cornfield rain. How thoroughly I have memorized the sound of that presence here, on this narrow cape, from years of rainwalk. I could lie in the dark anywhere, and hear it, and know whether or not I am home. I could walk in the night and tell you whether it was falling on the glossy shoulders of Little Sister Pond, or darkly and briskly on the longer fetch of Hatches Harbor.

And then, thinking of those *bodies of water*, I go mindroaming. I could name a hundred events, hours, creatures, that have filled me with delight, and fructifying praise. Experience! experience!—with the rain, and the trees, and all their kindred—has brought me a comfort and a modesty and a devotion to inclusiveness that I would not give up for all the gold in all the mountains of the world. This I knew, as I grew from simple delight toward thought and into conviction: such beauty as the earth offers must hold great meaning. So I began to consider the world as emblematic as well as real, and saw that it was—that shining word—virtuous. That it offers us, as surely as the wheat and the lilies grow, the dream of virtue.

I think of this every day. I think of it when I meet the turtle with its patient green face, or hear the hawk's tin-tongued skittering cry, or watch the otters at play in the pond. I am blood and bone however that happened, but I am convictions of my singular experience and my own thought, and they are made greatly of the hours of the earth, rough or smooth, but never less than intimate, poetic, dreamy, adamant, ferocious, loving, life-shaping.

Toward morning the rain slowed. I dressed and hurried out into the world.

Sand Dabs, Nine

The goose has finished laying her eggs. Of her exquisite dozen, the snapping turtle wants its share.

～

The owl is peaceful, until he is hungry.

～

Can you hear the voices of the ferns up-pushing, the little whippets of fresh air running through the trees?

～

The energy of attempt is greater than the surety of stasis.

～

Responsibility has tamed the phoebe.

～

All the eighth notes Mozart didn't have time to use before he entered the cloudburst, he gave to the wren.

～

Behind the glimmering cheerfulness of Bach there hangs a black thread.

～

The owl's face is like a feathered plate. Or, maybe, a judge.

～

No gift greater than ecstasy, unless it's patience.

～

The brawn, the silence, the thick crown of the black oak compose a life that is not to be despised.

～

In nature what looks like ornamentation is always of the greatest utility.

～

You too can be carved anew by the details of your devotions.

Home

A CERTAIN LUCENT correspondence has served me, all my life, in the ongoing search for my deepest thoughts and feelings. It is the relationship of my own mind to landscape, to the physical world—especially to that part of it with which, over the years, I have (and not casually) become intimate. It is no great piece of furniture in the universe—no Niagara, or rainforest, or Sahara. Yet it is beautiful, and it ripples in the weathers as lively as any outpouring from the Great Lakes.

In its minor turns, and tinsels, and daily changes, this landscape seems actually intent on providing pleasure, as indeed it does; in its *constancy*, its inexorable obedience to laws I cannot begin to imagine much less understand, it is still a richer companion—steady commentary against my own lesser moods—my flightiness, my indifferences, my mind and heart absences.

I mean, by such flightiness, something that feels unsatisfied at the center of my life—that makes me shaky, fickle, inquisitive, and hungry. I could call it a longing for home and not be far wrong. Or I could call it a longing for whatever supersedes, if it cannot pass through, understanding. Other words that come to mind: faith, grace, rest. In my outward appearance and life habits I hardly change—there's never been a day that my friends haven't been able to say, and at a distance, "There's Oliver, still standing around in the weeds. There she is, still scribbling in her notebook." But, at the center: I am shaking; I am flashing like tinsel. Restless, I read about ideas. Yet I let them remain ideas. I read about the poet who threw his books away, the better to come to a spiritual completion. Yet I keep my books. I flutter; I am attentive, maybe I even rise a little, balancing; then I fall back.

I don't however despair at such failures! I know I am sister to the dreamy-hearted dog who thinks only small thoughts; and to the green tree who thinks, perhaps, no thoughts at all, as well as to Rumi, and St. Francis. No, I don't mind the failures so long as I am still striving.

Which I am, and in this way. Daily I walk out across my landscape, the same fields, the same woods, and the same pale beaches; I stand beside the same blue and festive sea where the invisible winds, on late summer afternoons, are wound into huge, tense coils, and the waves put on their white feathers and begin to leap shoreward, to their last screaming and throbbing landfall. Times beyond remembering I have seen such moments: summer falling to fall, to be followed by what will follow: winter again: count on it. Opulent and ornate world, because at its root, and its axis, and its ocean bed, it swings through the universe *quietly* and *certainly*. It is: fun, and familiar, and healthful, and unbelievably refreshing, and lovely. And it is the theater of the spiritual; it is the multiform utterly obedient to a mystery.

And here I build a platform, and live upon it, and think my thoughts, and aim high. To rise, I must have a field to rise from. To deepen, I must have a bedrock from which to descend. The constancy of the physical world, under its green and blue dyes, draws me toward a better, richer self, call it elevation (there is hardly an adequate word), where I might ascend a little—where a gloss of spirit would mirror itself in worldly action. I don't mean just mild goodness. I mean feistiness too, the fires of human energy stoked; I mean a gladness vivacious enough to disarrange the sorrows of the world into something better. I mean whatever real rejoicing can do! We all know how brassy and wonderful it is to come into some new understanding. Imagine what it would be like, to lounge on the high ledge of submission and pure wonder. Nature, all around us, is our manifest exemplar. Not from the fox, or the leaf, or the drop of rain will you ever hear doubt or argument.

People say to me: wouldn't you like to see Yosemite? The Bay of Fundy? The Brooks Range? I smile and answer, "Oh yes—sometime," and go off to my woods, my ponds, my sun-filled harbor, no more than a blue comma on the map of the world but, to me, the emblem of everything. It is the intimate, never the general, that is teacherly. The idea of love is not love. The idea of ocean is neither salt nor sand; the face of the seal cannot rise from the *idea* to stare at you, to astound your heart. Time must grow thick and merry with incident, before thought can begin.

It is one of the perils of our so-called civilized age that we do not yet acknowledge enough, or cherish enough, this connection between soul and landscape—between our own best possibilities, and the view from our own windows. We need the world as much as it needs us, and we need it in privacy, intimacy, and surety. We need the field from which the lark rises—bird that is more than itself, that is the voice of the universe: vigorous, godly joy. Without the physical world such hope is: hacked off. Is: dried up. Without wilderness no fish could leap and flash, no deer could bound soft as eternal waters over the field; no bird could open its wings and become buoyant, adventurous, valorous beyond even the plan of nature. Nor could we.

Poem: Summer Night

The night is so long, its pages are so slow.
Who can read it?
Who can guess the final chapter,
or the afterword?

Moonlight is another story, of lovers mostly.
And starlight still another, of the heaven
we hope for in the haze of the heavens.

And there are little musics, sometimes,
as though the mockingbird, also, can't sleep.

If I step outside
I smell the grass, or the rain.
Or that purse of honey, another one awake—

the blue iris, so straight, so sweet-lipped.
Soft and alone in the dark.

Poem: Carrying the Snake to the Garden

In the cellar
was the smallest snake
I have ever seen.
It coiled itself
in a corner
and watched me
with eyes
like two little stars
set into coal,
and a tail
that quivered.
One step
of my foot
and it fled
like a running shoelace,
but a scoop of the wrist
and I had it
in my hand.
I was sorry
for the fear,
so I hurried
upstairs and out the kitchen door
to the warm grass
and the sunlight
and the garden.
It turned and turned
in my hand
but when I put it down

it didn't move.
I thought
it was going to flow
up my leg
and into my pocket.
I thought, for a moment,
as it lifted its face,
it was going to sing.

And then it was gone.

Poem: By the Wild-Haired Corn

I don't know
if the sunflowers
are angels always,
but surely sometimes.

Who, even in heaven,
wouldn't want to wear,
for awhile,
such a seed-face

and brave spine,
a coat of leaves
with so many pockets—
and who wouldn't want

to stand, for a summer day,
in the hot fields,
in the lonely country
of the wild-haired corn?

This much I know,
when I see the bright
stars of their faces,
when I'm strolling nearby,

I grow soft in my speech,
and soft in my thoughts,
and I remember how everything will be everything else,
by and by.

Where I Live

Now and again the earth begins to desire rest. And in the weeks of autumn especially it shows its disposition to calm, to what feels like a stasis, a pause. The ocean retains its warmth, while high, white cloud-boats ride out of the west. Now the birds of the woods are often quiet, but on the shore the migrating sanderlings and plovers are many and vocal, rafts of terns with the year's young among them come with the incoming tides, and plunge into the waves, and rise with silver leaves in their beaks. One can almost see the pulsing of their hearts, vigorous and tiny in the trim of white feathers. Where I live, on the harbor edge of the Cape's last town, perfect strangers walking along the beach turn and say to each other, without embarrassment or hesitation: *isn't it beautiful!*

Indeed it is. We are gifted wherever we look—the asters, the goldenrod along the highways have taken heaven's light, and dyed themselves with it, and so left us amid endless decoration. The first Eastham turnips—only as big as baseballs, but they will be larger in a few weeks—are sweet as honey. See them, piled on farm stands at the edge of the roads. And both the harbor-side and back-shore waves, brisk so long in the spring and summer, come now to shore like waves half-asleep. In the woods, the buck I have seen all summer in his red coat has gone to market and exchanged it for a plain brown one, warmer, for the coming months. Did I not see him also last year? And the year before? Suddenly it crosses the mind—the here and the now are, at the same time, the everywhere, and the forever.

I was born and raised far inland, but no matter. In the sixties I first saw Provincetown and declared myself a citizen who, however long I might live, would look every day into the sea's blue expanse. Now I have come to my forty-third year in this town. For all towns it has been a difficult and painful year. Yet the apples are crisp and firm, in the pinewoods where I walk every morning the mushrooms are plentiful, and creatively placed among the shining needles. I pick them and store them; all winter they feed us. Also cranberries—I mean the wild ones—are many and gleaming in the curly bogs. On the upper Cape the fields are long and wide, and stridently red, and cranberrying is an important business. For the gathering, workers use rakes, water, and machinery. In my own little bog I pick by hand, and with no haste. It is so pleasant in the afternoon light, what should compel me to hurry away? A few birds are still with us. The downy woodpecker's tinsel ribbon floats from a nearby oak, goldfinches, full of good humor, sing from a distant part of the sky. If a twig snaps and I raise my head slowly I will likely be looking into the gray eyes of the coyote who also, and as earnestly as I, is looking for his livelihood in this leafy place.

—

Somewhere among the wonderful writings of H. V. Morton is the thought—I don't remember the exact wording—that it is difficult, indeed impossible, to reconcile landscape, its grandeur and its serenity, with history. Morton wrote this while traveling in Italy, where he found that country's natural beauty perpetually before him, and where there is plenty of history. But it is true everywhere, and even here on this silky fringe of land only a few thousand years old, for life is as much in the mind as in the eye, and no grievous event therefore is blotted out by distance. But I think we do better than most places. There is a tradition on the Cape, and in my town especially, of patience, and openness to change. There is plenty of attachment to the past, and voices can flare over the destruction of an old building or the reorientation of roads, or the cutting down of trees, but at the end there appears a willingness to go forward, to accept the differences that must be, without collision.

We know there are more people coming, every year, to our personal paradise. No one, however, has yet suggested we close the bridge. And not only because of the commercial gain realized from tourism, but, I think, out of a sense of fairness—what we have in plenty, and all year, surely should be available to everyone, at least for a while. Moreover, there is always the hope and the chance that the astonishing natural beauty here will open the heart, of both tourist and resident, to a new striving after virtue; such immutable suggestive power the natural world has always had, and offers to each of us. And certainly this experience belongs to everyone, along with all the other experiences of the Cape—its art, its history, its commerce, its good food, its fun and fevers, its rambunctiousness. Here are the ocean and wild dunes, here is downtown, here is my own bird-voiced cranberry bog. So the effort goes on—to accommodate more people, yet to keep the reasons they want to come here intact.

Autumn lasts only a few weeks, easing in brightly colored, then darkening, like the ponds back of town. The terns are gone. The white peaks and coils of the back-shore waves, waking again, make their rousing suggestions of a colder and harder time on the way. Now restaurants forget their icy desserts and begin to elaborate the chowders, the baked beans, the hot cider. How many people have found some memorable experience and pleasure here, from the broad reach of dune and marshland, from the hills of Truro, from the sea sparkle?

One fall day I come home from the woods and drive downtown to pick up the mail. A town crew are removing the No Parking signs, some of the men with familiar voices and faces, the sons of Provincetown people I knew forty years ago. Then the truck moves on. It is late afternoon, just a glimmer of the softest, quietest darkness in the air. When I descend the post office steps I can feel, even here, a little sand under my shoes. And the long street, stringing west and east past so many shop windows, restaurant doors, pots of flowers, houses unchanged from a hundred years ago or standing in their renewed finery, is, for a moment, empty.

Poem: Waking on a Summer Morning

Water
skidding down platforms of stone
ten miles
nothing to talk to but ferns

in the deep water
the eye of a trout
under a shelf of stone
not moving

no one will ever sully the water
the ferns will go on sleeping and dreaming
no one will ever find the trout
for a thousand years he may lie there, gleaming.

Prose Poem: One Winter Day

Today the floes came. They made their stately approach with the incoming tide, in no hurry but as if destined. The tide fell and they were left like dropped clouds along the beach. Little boys clambered onto them, as though they were white ships that could carry them out to sea. The gulls and the eiders also seemed to feel they were here for entertainment, and chose to rest upon this or that shining pinnacle. Those still in water were no more than islands, but when left on shore they revealed themselves entirely, huge, and as gorgeously shaped as sculpture, both inspired and fortunate. A blue light glowed from their crevices. They might have been souls.

Notes

Mary Oliver dedicated all three books to her partner, Molly Malone Cook.

From THE LEAF AND THE CLOUD

Archive Note: Oliver's Acknowledgments

My thanks to the editors of the following magazines, in which sections of this poem have previously appeared.

>   *DoubleTake:* From The Book of Time
>   *Five Points:* Evening Star
>   *The Ohio Review:* Riprap
>   *Shenandoah:* Flare
>   *The Southern Review:* Work
>   *The Virginia Quarterly Review:* Gravel

"Flare" received the 1998 James Boatwright III Prize for Poetry; my thanks to *Shenandoah*.

"Flare" also appears in *The Best American Poetry 1999*, published by Scribner.

"Work" also appears in *The Best American Poetry 2000*, published by Scribner.

And my deepest appreciation to the Lannan Foundation for their gift of a 1998 Lannan Literary Award.

From WHAT DO WE KNOW

Archive Note: Oliver's Acknowledgments

I thank the editors of the following magazines, in which, sometimes in a slightly different form, some of the poems in this volume were first published.

> *The American Scholar:* Clam, The Loon
> *Appalachia:* Raven with Crows, Wind
> *Cape Cod Voice:* Blue Iris, The Roses
> *Cybernetics and Human Knowing:* Summer Poem
> *DoubleTake:* Black Snake, Mockingbird
> *Five Points:* Heron Rises from the Dark, Summer Pond; Last Night the Rain Spoke to Me; Tree Sparrows; Walking to Oak-Head Pond, and Thinking of the Ponds I Will Visit in the Next Days and Weeks
> *Image:* Moonlight, Snowy Night, Stones, The Word
> *Michigan Quarterly Review:* On Losing a House
> *Shenandoah:* Beauty, Oranges
> *The Southern Review:* Sometimes I Am Victorious and Even Beautiful, Their Wings
> *Witness:* Gratitude, Mink
> Crows, Early Snow, One Hundred White-sided Dolphins on a Summer Day, and Winter at Herring Cove originally appeared in *The New Yorker.*

From LONG LIFE

Hawthorne's *Mosses from an Old Manse*

1. Emerson says the room where he wrote was on the second floor, facing northwest. Hawthorne also speaks of a northwest room, that looked "down into the orchard."

2. The "w" in Hawthorne was added to the original spelling by Nathaniel the writer.

3. From *English Men of Letters,* edited by John Morley (New York: Harper and Brothers, 1887). The long chapter on Hawthorne was written by Henry James, Jr., as he was known at that time.

4. *The Memoirs of Julian Hawthorne,* edited by Edith Garrigues Hawthorne (New York: Macmillan, 1938), 158–159.

5. Hawthorne and Franklin Pierce (U.S. president from 1853–1857) began a lifelong friendship while both were at Bowdoin College.

Sand Dabs

1. The first six "Sand Dabs" are in the previous books *Blue Pastures, West Wind,* and *Winter Hours.* The sand dab is a small, bony, not very significant but well-put-together fish.

Archive Note: Oliver's Acknowledgments

Some of the writings in *Long Life* have previously appeared in magazines or books, as follows. My thanks to all editors.

"Flow"—*Shenandoah*
"Dog Talk"—*Seneca Review*
"The Perfect Days"—*Appalachia*
"Waste Land: An Elegy"—*Orion*

"Emerson: An Introduction," "Hawthorne's *Mosses from an Old Manse,*" and "*The House of the Seven Gables*" were written as introductions for the Modern Library Classics series published by Random House. All three of these volumes have been published.

"Are You Okay?"—*Five Points*
"Dust"—*Shenandoah.* Dust also appeared in *The Best American Essays, 2001,* series editor Robert Atwan.
"The Morning Walk"—*Appalachia*
"Comfort"—*Onearth*
"Home"—*Aperture*
"Where I Live"—*Boston Magazine*
"Waking on a Summer Morning"—*Onearth*
"Softest of Mornings"—*Cape Cod Voice*

Acknowledgments

In the acknowledgments of all her books, Mary Oliver exclusively thanks the editors who first published her poems. Here, I'd like to thank her for creating a canon so timeless and transcendent that people of all ages, backgrounds, and faiths can find peace in just a few lines, and I'd like to thank the little village that brought this book to life.

Thanks to the first editor of this project Mollie Weisenfeld for digging these books out of Hachette's backlist and contracting this work, as well as Jesseca Salky Agency and the estate NW Orchard for allowing this book to be. Bill, Clarissa, Jesseca, Mairead, thank you for securing Oliver's legacy. Thank you, Natalie Diaz for opening this space in every human's hands, and thank you, dear reader, for your time and your mind.

Further behind the curtain, many thanks to the production editor Cisca Schreefel, proofreader Lori Hobkirk, and interior designer Bart Dawson. And speaking of design, thank you to Amanda Kain for the limitless cover, Eoghan Kavanagh for the photograph, and Liz Connor for shepherding it through to print. Thanks also to our other teammates, managing editor Rebecca Holland, production coordinator Emily Baker, manufacturing coordinator Maisa Nammari, and Dan Lynch on galleys, and over in sound, audio editor Laura Essex, producer Melanie Schmidt, engineer Joey Buttafuoco, post-production supervisors Lara Ziccardi and Michael Bader, and narrator

Kimberly Farr. Thank you Alana Spendley in marketing and Gina DiBenedetto in publicity, as well as our entire sales force and sub-rights colleagues both national and international, for spreading the word. Thank you to our fulfilment team in Indiana for taking stock and shipping out; thank you to the countless bookstores, booksellers, librarians, reviewers, and teachers of all stripes for sharing; and of course, gratitude to various heads of capital that have supported this book's creation.

Little Alleluias is a midlife masterpiece—so to end as we begin: thank you, Mary Oliver, for your insight and grace, for teaching us how to belong to a land that belongs to itself, and for guiding us through the light and dark and rainbowed clothes of the world.

Niyati
Editor, *Little Alleluias*
March 8, 2025

About the Author

Credit: © 2005 Rachel Giese Brown

Born in a small town in Ohio, **Mary Oliver** published her first book of poetry in 1963 at the age of 28. Over the course of her long career, she received numerous awards. Her fourth book, *American Primitive,* won the Pulitzer Prize for Poetry in 1984. She led workshops and held residencies at various colleges and universities, including Bennington College, where she held the Catharine Osgood Foster Chair for Distinguished Teaching. Oliver died in 2019.